D0052623

WHAT
DA VINCI
DIDN'T KNOW

WHAT
DA VINCI
DIDN'T KNOW

AN LDS PERSPECTIVE

Richard Neitzel Holzapfel
Andrew C. Skinner
Thomas A. Wayment

DESERET
BOOK

SALT LAKE CITY, UTAH

To Nathan and Irene, my son and daughter-in-law—RNH

To Janet, my true confidante—ACS

In memory of my grandfather, Arvel Edwin Stratford
(September 7, 1916—September 29, 2001)—TAW

© 2006 Richard Neitzel Holzapfel, Andrew C. Skinner, Thomas A. Wayment

All rights reserved. No part of this book may be reproduced in any form or by any means without permission in writing from the publisher, Deseret Book Company, P. O. Box 30178, Salt Lake City, Utah 84130. This work is not an official publication of The Church of Jesus Christ of Latter-day Saints. The views expressed herein are the responsibility of the authors and do not necessarily represent the position of the Church or of Deseret Book Company.

DESERET BOOK is a registered trademark of Deseret Book Company.

Visit us at deseretbook.com

Library of Congress Cataloging-in-Publication Data
Holzapfel, Richard Neitzel.
    What Da Vinci didn't know : an LDS perspective / Richard Neitzel Holzapfel, Andrew C. Skinner, and Thomas A. Wayment.
        p.   cm.
    Includes bibliographical references and index.
    ISBN-10 1-59038-608-6 (pbk.)
    ISBN-13 978-1-59038-608-8 (pbk.)
    1. Brown, Dan, 1964– Da Vinci code.   2. Jesus Christ—In literature.
3. Mary Magdalene, Saint—In literature.   4. Christian saints in literature.
5. Christianity in literature.   I. Skinner, Andrew C., 1951–   II. Wayment,
Thomas A.   III. Title.
    PS3552.R685434D3344   2006
    813'.54—dc22   2006008166

Printed in the United States of America
Worzalla Publishing Co., Stevens Point, WI

10   9   8   7   6   5   4   3   2   1

Contents

Acknowledgments

We are thankful for several individuals who helped us complete this project in a timely and thoughtful manner. First, we appreciate the following individuals at Deseret Book: Cory H. Maxwell (publisher), Richard Peterson (editor), Richard Erickson (designer), and Tonya Facemyer (typesetter).

Alison Coutts, our friend and colleague at BYU, transcribed handwritten versions and prepared electronic copies of two chapters. Ted D. Stoddard, our constant supporter, colleague, and friend, edited every chapter several times from first draft through final draft, providing not only his good writing skills but also asking thoughtful questions and raising points about the content as well. Joseph B. Hinckley, our competent and friendly BYU student research assistant, gathered primary resources and finished identifying, ordering, and organizing the images in the book.

We are also grateful to Steve Bule, Professor of Art and Humanities, Utah Valley State College, Orem, Utah. Steve specializes in Italian Renaissance art history, with a Ph.D. from Ohio State University and is a fellow returned missionary from Italy. His help and mentoring for the essay in chapter 6, "Leonardo's *The*

Last Supper," not only saved us from factual errors but also enriched our discussion of the subject.

Finally, we are grateful to Ronald and Linda Lindsey for their generous donation to BYU, which covered the expenses related to the purchase and permissions-use fees for all of the images included in our project.

Introduction

"The Bible represents a fundamental guidepost for millions of people on the planet. . . . Those who truly understand their faiths understand the stories are metaphorical."

(*The Da Vinci Code*, p. 342)

Winston Churchill said, "In history lie all the secrets." Though he was speaking of statecraft, his comment is equally applicable to matters of religion. That is, within the context of faith, history can provide answers to important religious questions. In fact, our scriptures are narratives that are grounded in history and that contain the secrets to life itself. And our spiritual enlightenment can often be increased when the scriptures are interpreted by inspired writers and prophets who go to the past to explain the mighty deeds of God.

One of the basic questions we address in this short book is What truths can we find in historical novels that are sold in the fiction section of bookstores but that nevertheless claim to be rooted in history and based on original sources?

Obviously, based on the sheer number of dollars spent, members of our society are often much more interested in getting their history lessons from novels, television shows, and Hollywood movies than through the traditional outlet in which competent historians provide scholarly explorations of the past. Scholars and academics who have forgotten the "story" in history are partly responsible for the lack of interest in and support of their histori-cal craft because their works are often stilted, unimaginative, and basically uninteresting.

Exceptions abound, such as David McCullough's *John Adams* (2001) and *1776* (2005). Both efforts prove that historical works can be meticulously researched, well-written, and also extremely interesting.

Neither historical novels nor popular films are inherently inadequate in presenting history to a wide audience. The outcome is not a case of good versus bad when these two media outlets choose to tell a story from the past. The questions all of us may raise, however, are about the authors' and screenwriters' fidelity to original sources and their careful and thoughtful interpretation of the historical record. Using that criteria, we have chosen to focus our attention on Dan Brown's best-selling book, *The Da Vinci Code* (New York: Doubleday, 2003).

The Da Vinci Code is a fast-paced, suspenseful thriller set amid the landscapes, museums, and cathedrals of Europe. The novel takes us initially into the Musée du Louvre in Paris where we discover that one of the curators, Jacques Saunière, has been mur-dered. However, before he dies, Saunière is able to leave clues—not about his death but about a secret that will shake the very foundation of Christianity and the Catholic Church. We then are introduced to Sophie Neveu, the murdered curator's granddaugh-ter and a cryptologist, and Robert Langdon, a visiting Harvard professor, both of whom have been called to the murder scene for various reasons. The two, who will become romantically involved along the way, are swept through a long night of murders and intrigue that continues with a police chase out of Paris to a wet morning in London. As the mystery unfolds, they discover, with the help of Sir Leigh Teabing, British historian and noted Grail scholar, that the great secret associated with the murders and intrigue deals with Jesus of Nazareth. They also discover that

Leonardo da Vinci

Leonardo da Vinci (1452–1519), Self-Portrait, Biblioteca Reale, Turin, Italy. According to *The Da Vinci Code,* Leonardo was Grand Master of the Priory of Sion from 1510 to 1519, one of the oldest secret societies on earth and custodian of the knowledge concerning the Holy Grail. *Used by Permission, Nimatallah/Art Resource, NY*

Vatican

Aerial view of St. Peter's basilica with Piazza S. Pietro and the Vatican Palaces in Vatican City. The center of intrigue in *The Da Vinci Code,* the Vatican—representing Christendom—is purported to have actively tried to suppress the earliest stories of Jesus of Nazareth that revealed Him to be nothing more than a mortal man. *Used by Permission, Alinari/Art Resource, NY*

Sophie's grandfather was part of the group that has been custodians of the explosive secret for generations—the Priory of Sion. In England, the identity of the evil "Teacher" who masterminded the murders committed by an albino monk from *Opus Dei* is revealed, and the story reaches its climax.

During the fast-paced race to the finish, Sophie learns that Jesus was mortal, not divine; that He was married to Mary Magdalene, who stood at the cross pregnant; that the earliest gospels, and therefore the most reliable, are not those found in the current New Testament; and that the Catholic Church has attempted through murder, lies, and deceit to hide these facts from the masses since the earliest times of its existence.

Sophie and Robert also discover that the guardians of this great secret (the true identity of Christ and the role of women in the early Church), the Priory of Sion, have included such prestigious members as Leonardo da Vinci, Botticelli, Sir Isaac Newton, and Victor Hugo, all of whom have possessed and passed down through the generations this secret knowledge, as well as the true identity of the Holy Grail. In particular, Leonardo da Vinci is said to have left clues in his artwork that if deciphered could lead someone to the ultimate truth. Sophie and Robert also learn that this super-secret and powerful group continued the practices of ancient rituals that celebrate the sacred feminine—something ruthlessly suppressed by the Vatican since the time of the pagan emperor Constantine.

The Da Vinci Code is the "rarest of birds," both a critical and a commercial success, with tens of millions of copies sold and with translations in more than forty languages. The book is also a historic publication. As *Harry Potter* turned out to be the book to be read by today's young people, *The Da Vinci Code* has become the must-read for adults. Its continued availability in hardcover is the result of its amazing endurance on the *New York Times* Best Seller List.

The book's initial print run of a mere eighty-five thousand copies has been multiplied astronomically. Ongoing interest in *The Da Vinci Code* has spawned various television specials, popular museum tours to England and France, countless book reviews, numerous articles and books by various individuals responding to the claims put forth in the novel, and a major Hollywood movie based on the book's storyline.

The reason for all the excitement is obviously more than the simple economic bottom line. The book has been read by tens of millions, exposing them to a revisionist view of Jesus of Nazareth that has caught the media's attention as well as the attention of committed Christians and scholars. Surprising to some is the fact that some of the viewpoints put forth in *The Da Vinci Code* were originally outlined by scholars. The novel, in fact, incorporates many scholarly views, subtly adapted into its storyline. Ultimately, *The Da Vinci Code* demonstrates society's current intense interest in religious history and its continuing fascination with a historical Jesus.

We are not endorsing this immensely popular book. Neither are we encouraging nor discouraging anyone's reading it or seeing the movie. However, the media attention surrounding the book's publication and now its additional life as a major motion picture invites us to explore the book's issues in the light of the New Testament texts, the history of Christianity as a religion, and the debate over the discoveries and rediscoveries of a plethora of old texts claiming to preserve stories related to Jesus, His Church, and the true gospel of Christ.

What we may forget in the heat and passion of the historical and theological debate about the contents of the book and film is the fact that the book is a work of fiction. In fact, following the title of the book on the dust jacket and title page is found the description, "A Novel." A problem arises with those words, however, because *The Da Vinci Code* qualifies the subtitle, "A Novel," and dogmatically and categorically states, "All descriptions of artwork, architecture, documents, and secret rituals in this novel are accurate" (*The Da Vinci Code,* p. 1).

Because of *The Da Vinci Code*'s claims to accuracy, the book may be evaluated in the same rigorous and careful way any other scholarly endeavor might be examined—that is, scrutinized in light of the available historical sources and established evidence.

However, this examination of the claims made in the novel is not intended to be an exhaustive, scholarly endeavor. Indeed, in an effort to make our book more reader-friendly, a minimum of footnotes have been provided. Those who wish to explore the subject in more depth are referred to the bibliography that has been provided.

Clearly, given the number and vigor of various discussions with individuals on airplanes, at social events, in university class-rooms, and in the hallways at religious gatherings, we think *The Da Vinci Code* raises some important questions that are worth examining.

Although living in societies that are influenced by the Judeo-Christian tradition, Christians today are generally woefully unin-formed about the radical academic forces that are determined to reinterpret the basic and long-standing traditions about Jesus of Nazareth and the early Christian movement that declared Him to be the divine Son of God.

For a long while, the topics discussed and debated by New Testament scholars in academic conferences and in scholarly jour-nals and books, which may have caused the blood of the faithful to "boil," were reserved for the academy—behind the closed doors of white ivory towers. Recently, some of these radical scholars have been successful in presenting their ideas to an increasingly larger audience, without using the typical scholarly jargon that masked their findings and without the scholarly reviews that usually attend academic publishing. In this larger audience are lay consumers who are not typically inclined to ask thoughtful, penetrating ques-tions about sources or the interpretation of those sources. And the academic press has been replaced by a new outlet—the popular media, whose interests are not always unbiased but rather are driven by ratings and revenue.

After spending several years responding to questions raised in popular outlets, the authors of this book began paying attention to what family, friends, and students were reading and watching. We were surprised at the number of programs found on the History and Discovery television channels and the frequency of reports in *Newsweek, Time,* and *U.S. News & World Report* about

Jesus and the early Christian Church. Although often visually stimulating and cleverly presented, many of these programs and reports, we felt, were profoundly influenced by a fringe of radical scholars bent on rewriting the past.

In the face of numerous questions specifically related to *The Da Vinci Code*'s premises and assertions, we finally purchased and read our own copies of this runaway bestseller. Although we recognized the book's literary merits and could appreciate the suspense generated by its intriguing plot, we also instantly knew that *The Da Vinci Code* was the latest and most successful attempt to provide an alternative interpretation of Jesus of Nazareth and early Christianity. We could also see that it drew heavily upon the provocative arguments and conclusions set forth by radical New Testament scholars, who have dedicated their lives to redefining who Jesus was and what He did.

From the countless questions from our friends and associates, we know *The Da Vinci Code* has generated a lot of interest among Latter-day Saints. Interestingly, we came to discover also that Christians in general (who are divided on some essential issues about church authority and the divine nature of Christ) are typically united in their praise of *The Da Vinci Code*. What seemed obvious to us is that helpful responses to the fundamental questions raised in the book needed to be provided.

For some readers, *The Da Vinci Code* freed them from conventional rules and values because the book provided an attack on the establishment and the traditional claims of Christianity—claims that constitute the "good news," or the gospel of Christ. It also challenged attitudes about women and priesthood, Church authority, and divine miracles, especially the Atonement and the Resurrection.

In an effort to help clarify the issues involved, we, including our colleague Eric D. Huntsman, initially participated in a recorded discussion entitled "What Da Vinci Didn't Know: LDS

Perspectives on the *Code*," released through Deseret Book (2004). None of us imagined at the time that we would follow up with a book about *The Da Vinci Code*. However, after a flood of interesting and passionate conversations, letters, e-mails, and telephone calls in response to our CD, each of us began to think about how we might respond more completely to some of the important issues raised by *The Da Vinci Code*.

Proposals for the publication of a book were independently submitted to Deseret Book, without any of the present authors being aware of what the others had done. Deseret Book's Cory Maxwell contacted us to ask if we would be willing to work together on one project that would further the discussion. With a tight deadline, we agreed to do so, and we outlined a book that we thought would address the important issues raised by *The Da Vinci Code*.

In light of the continued commercial success of the hardback edition of *The Da Vinci Code*, the release of a "Special Illustrated Edition" (2004), a two-million-copy paperback edition (2006), and a Hollywood movie based on the book (2006), our decision was most likely a fortuitous one.

Actually, our real interest is focused on neither Dan Brown's novel nor Ron Howard's film. Although they provide the basis of our discussion, they are simply a springboard to reconsider, once again, the life and ministry of Jesus Christ. The popularity of the book and movie also affords us an opportunity to discuss the events that followed Jesus' suffering, death, and resurrection—events that profoundly impacted Western culture and society when a written canon was finally compiled that provides the basis for Christians' beliefs about Jesus of Nazareth.

Based on our observations during the last several years, three themes or topics from *The Da Vinci Code* seem to have captured the attention of a number of Latter-day Saints.

First, the book is anti-Catholic and unfairly, in many

instances, characterizes the history, beliefs, and practices of the Catholic Church, past and present. Some Latter-day Saints, like our Protestant neighbors, have been influenced negatively in their attitudes toward Rome, the papacy, and the Catholic Church because of the dominant Protestant culture. American prejudice against the largest Christian denomination in the world began during the colonial period of our history—transported from Europe where the conflict between Protestantism and Catholicism was particularly intense.

Second, the book describes secret texts and an elaborate conspiracy to hide the content of those texts from the masses. Some Latter-day Saints, because of the remarkable stories of the coming forth of the Book of Mormon and the Book of Abraham, have been eager to accept accounts that, in their minds and without careful investigation, seem to validate our Church's claims of additional scripture. Like other Americans, some LDS readers have been willing to accept at face value the conspiracy theories about almost anything involving textual cover-ups—again without careful and thoughtful review.

Finally, the book's main secret revolves around marriage—in this case the presumed marriage of Jesus of Nazareth and Mary of Magdala (known as Mary Magdalene). Our interest in the subject derives from our Church's focus on marriage as a most important and sacred practice. Additionally, even though not an official doctrine of the Church, some Latter-day Saints have speculated that Jesus may have been married to fulfill all righteousness (see Genesis 2:24).

Many Latter-day Saints who are intrigued by this novel seemingly forget that the Jesus who is finally revealed at the end of *The Da Vinci Code* is not the Jesus of Matthew, Mark, Luke, and John. He is not the Messiah; He is not the Son of God; and He is not the divine Redeemer of the world. At best, *The Da Vinci Code's* Jesus was a wise man, maybe even a prophet, but He is not the suffering, dying Savior of the world who was miraculously raised from death by God on the first day of the week.

As noted above, the focus in this book, *What Da Vinci Didn't Know,* is not on Dan Brown's book itself as much as on some of the important questions raised in *The Da Vinci Code.* Therefore, we hope our book will be helpful to those who have read Dan Brown's novel or seen Ron Howard's film as well as to those who have neither read the book nor seen the film.

Ultimately, we see our efforts as part of a much larger dialogue with family members, friends, neighbors, and other people about Jesus and the scriptures. The resulting discussion, we strongly feel, will prove that faithful and thoughtful Latter-day Saints have something to contribute to a world searching for answers to important questions in these challenging times, as reflected in Timothy's prophecy: "This know also, that in the last days perilous times shall come. . . . [Men and women shall be] ever learning, and never able to come to the knowledge of the truth" (2 Timothy 3:1, 7).

CHAPTER 1

Approaching History:
The Da Vinci Code As a Case Study

"All descriptions of artwork, architecture,
documents, and secret rituals in this novel are accurate."

(*The Da Vinci Code,* p. 1)

We live in the hectic present. Daily concerns take almost every moment of our attention, and we still have unfinished business when we finally go to sleep. Yet in those rare moments when we free ourselves of the present, we naturally, almost instinctively, worry and dream about the future, leaving little room for anything else.

Interest in the Past

Because we live in the present and dream of the future, the question naturally arises, Why should we be interested in the past, especially the distant past? The past is elusive. The records left to us are fragmentary and often contradictory. Even the most interested among us are often quite conflicted about how to interpret the past. Decades of historical inquiry have at least made two points—that the past is in some way a "foreign place" and that we will forever be attempting to fully understand it.

Additionally, we may ask ourselves, Because life is short and uncertain, thus making time a precious commodity, should we

1

waste it in the past when there is so much in the present and the approaching future that captures our attention?

For many religiously devoted individuals, some events of the past hold obvious significance—particularly the life and ministry of Jesus Christ. Nevertheless, even among dedicated disciples, most are interested only in the narrow focus of Jesus' life, death, and resurrection. Beyond that, history stimulates little interest among most people. This lack of interest probably arises because few people understand how to approach history in a way that makes it meaningful for them.

Two Important Skills

Part of the reason we struggle with the past is that parents and teachers rarely transmit two important skills of historical inquiry: (1) respectful questioning and (2) a wonder and openness about the past.

By "respectful questioning," we mean two things. First, we should realize that we are dealing with real people from the past who were acting in real time. We must respect them as individuals. We must be more sympathetic and less judgmental than we often are when we judge historical figures from our modern perspective. Second, we cannot be gullible and thereby accept every interpretation of historical events and historical figures at face value. This outcome is often an issue with popular media portrayals of the past. For any article, book, television program, or Hollywood movie, we need to ask questions about the sources used, the intentions of the author, and the context of the production.

The second skill is having "a wonder and openness about the past." By this, we mean we must be ready to experience the excitement and thrill of learning lessons from the past. Additionally, we must be open and flexible in dealing with new interpretations and new information. A new discovery can add depth and breadth to our understanding of the present as well as the past. Tunnel vision has no place in legitimate historical inquiry.

The harmonious marriage of these two skills within the mind of every person should be one of the primary goals of education. We recognize that, in some ways, they seem to be conflicting modes of thought, but they are imperative to effective historical inquiry. We must strike a balance. At a time when popular culture is offering us provocative portraits of important people and events—among them Jesus of Nazareth and Mary Magdalene—we face no more important history lesson than teaching these skills.

Popular History

Our current culture tends to be ahistorical—that is, not concerned with history or with historical development. For the most part, we have not been accustomed to the skills needed to carefully and thoughtfully engage the past. As professors of religious education at Brigham Young University, we often meet excited individuals who want to share with us their interpretations of the past, which are usually views that are more informed by pop perception than by careful historical inquiry. Such individuals are often widely read and know various speculative nuances of popular history. *The Da Vinci Code,* or some other popular interpretation of the past, has captured their attention, and they are eager to talk with a university professor about their views.

Notice the kinds of questions that have been asked us in response to "*The Da Vinci Code* phenomenon":

1. Do you believe the Catholic Church is hiding documents in the Vatican?

2. Do you believe Jesus was married?

3. Do you believe the Nag Hammadi texts and the Dead Sea Scrolls contain truths that have been revealed in the Restoration?

4. Do you believe the European royal lines descend from Jesus?

It is interesting how such questions are phrased, suggesting that the questioners are dealing with a matter of belief and not of evidence. We are almost never asked, "How good is the evidence that Jesus was married?" or "What evidence do we have that the Nag Hammadi texts taught eternal marriage?"

In responding to these kinds of questions, we often notice that the excitement fades when we raise questions about some pop historical reconstruction that has been built more on imagination than on solid historical foundations and that has not gone through the rigors of peer review and debate. Sometimes we find that we are dismissing not just some errant historical conclusion but rather a theory that has become a precious facet of a reader's inner life, having given him or her some sort of "gnosis" or special knowledge. Somehow, pop history, obtained with little effort or thought, helps some people define themselves and their relationship to others.

Our encounters consist not only of providing answers to questions but also of replacing misunderstandings with something much more satisfying and thoughtful. There is, after all, so much in real history that is equally exciting, more mysterious, more intellectually challenging, and a lot closer to the truth than can be found in popular interpretations of history.

Individuals who thrive on history are often eloquent, intelligent, and curious. They have a natural appetite for discovering the wonders of the past. The problem is that real history has often been filtered in a way to make it more palatable before it reaches them. Our cultural motifs, our educational systems, and our communication media have failed us. What society permits to trickle through about the past is often something sensational or simply false.

Spurious accounts that snare the gullible are readily available. The Internet, the media, including national publishers, and the

History and Discovery television channels are the primary pur-
veyors of this kind of history today. As professors, we are
constantly bombarded with inquiries regarding some Internet
article, new book, or television program that is either sensational
or salacious. Certainly this is the case with *The Da Vinci Code,* a
book that, more often than not, gets its facts wrong and therefore
puts forth unsubstantiated conclusions of the past as though they
were "gospel truths."

A few flagrant examples will suffice to prove this point. Here
are some of the most egregious historical errors in *The Da Vinci
Code:*

1. There were more than eighty gospel accounts "considered
for the New Testament" by the early church (p. 231).

2. The New Testament canon was decided upon by a "pagan
Roman emperor Constantine the Great" (p. 231).

3. Jesus was not considered divine but was "viewed by his followers as a mortal prophet . . . a great and powerful man, but a
man nonetheless. A mortal," until the Council of Nicea in the
fourth century (p. 233).

4. The Dead Sea Scrolls were first discovered in the 1950s
(p. 234).

5. The Catholic Church "tried very hard to suppress the
release of" the Nag Hammadi codices (which *The Da Vinci Code*
mistakenly identifies as the "Coptic scrolls") (p. 234).

6. The Dead Sea Scrolls are "the earliest Christian records"
(p. 245).

7. Mary Magdalene was from "the House of Benjamin"
(p. 248).

8. "Mary Magdalene was pregnant at the time of the crucifixion" and was taken secretly to France by Jesus' "trusted uncle,
Joseph of Arimathea" (p. 255).

Dozens of similar blatantly false or completely unsubstantiated statements are found throughout *The Da Vinci Code.*

Ironically, the novel's title is a telling story itself. Leonardo was never known as "da Vinci." Like Jesus of Nazareth, his name tells us where he is from: Leonardo, "of Vinci," a small town in the heart of Tuscany.

Approaching the *Code*

The following question necessarily arises: Is it possible for individuals who are not necessarily pursuing a Ph.D. in history but who are genuinely interested in the past to be able to quickly detect the flawed historical context provided by a historical novel or a motion picture?

As intriguing as some pseudo-history may seem and as confident as we may be that we would never be so gullible as to be swept up by such doctrine, we know it is happening all around us. Pseudo-history attracts large numbers of accomplished people, even some with advanced degrees. For example, in looking at *The Da Vinci Code* as a case study, we must consider the following important points in assessing the facts: First, *The Da Vinci Code* purports that a secret cache of documents exists that contains information about Jesus and His alleged spouse Mary Magdalene. To make such a claim, we would either have had to view those documents or to know where they could be found. If such records are so readily available to the author, then we would want to know if they are available to others. Second, are there external historical sources that confirm the existence of such documents? The documents may exist, but that does not prove that they are ancient. They may indeed be forgeries. A reference to these documents from outside the collection would help confirm their existence. Third, does the internal logic of the account make sense—that is, can they be placed in a known historical setting?

For example, we might ask why the Catholic Church would suppress documents about Jesus' marriage when that information in itself is not problematic to their theology. Or we might ask why there were followers of Jesus during Constantine's reign who thought that Jesus was merely a human prophet. If He was nothing more than a married man who lived in the first century, then why did anyone follow Him? Finally, if the story as told in *The Da Vinci Code* is correct, then why did so many of the alleged conspirators leave clues to the world?

To ascertain the accuracy of historical claims, scholars and students must ask important questions such as those given above. Conclusions are sometimes not as important as how those conclusions were obtained, and the insightful investigator will ask not whether Jesus was married but rather if there is any credible information from His lifetime that suggests whether He was or was not.

History carries us toward an understanding of how the world *is* rather than how we might wish it to be. Encountering well-written, accurate history invariably elicits a sense of reverence and awe. Good history is refreshingly un-self-serving, circumspect, and understated.

Real history is astonishing. Real history is a delight. We are amazed at the prospects. Ultimately, history allows people long dead to talk directly to us. The books that record history can accompany us everywhere. Books are patient where we are slow to understand; they allow us to go over the difficult parts as many times as we wish, and they are never critical of our lapses. Books are the key to understanding the world.

In the end, our unending quest continues to be a journey of "discovery" as we visit that foreign land called the past. Further, our unending quest is also an effort to pass along the skills that will allow those who follow to embrace the past. Finally, we want to provide others a sense of discovery—the thrill of the journey.

Ultimately, we must create the delicate balance between

no-holds-barred openness and the most rigorous, respectful, questioning scrutiny. In the end, this approach will allow us to discover ourselves as we discover the world around us—including the past that has contributed to our present.

CHAPTER 2

Suppression of Texts within Early Christianity

"More than *eighty* gospels were considered for the New Testament, and yet only a relative few were chosen for inclusion— Matthew, Mark, Luke, and John among them."

(*The Da Vinci Code,* p. 231)

Unfortunately, we do not have any original manuscripts of either the Old or the New Testament. Therefore, we are left with copies of what the New Testament authors originally wrote. No doubt, some scholars are more skeptical than others about the historical accuracy of the documents known as the New Testament. Even so, we have legitimate historical reasons for believing that the New Testament contains the earliest existing written records concerning the life of Jesus. Whether other writings existed at one time, writings that have now been either lost or suppressed, is a matter of great interest. Today, distinct traces remain of the process by which certain books were excluded from the Bible and by which other books came to be included. Of course, all of us would like to find a cache of documents that were written earlier than our New Testament texts but which for unknown reasons were excluded from the canon.

The Earliest Writings about Jesus of Nazareth

One of the primary ways to discover whether other books contemporary with or earlier than the books contained in our

New Testament existed is to identify references to or quotations from lost books of scripture in the writings of early authors whose works have survived. Whether the authors were themselves Christians is not materially important. What is important is whether they knew of or could quote from early Christian sources. For this study, it is also important to note, where possible, what those sources taught about Jesus. Some scholars have advocated that the earliest sources about Jesus taught that He was nothing more than a mortal prophet who died a tragic death; but the earliest available sources, in fact, declare His divinity.

Fortunately, many authors in the late first and early second centuries knew of earlier Christian writings and quoted from them, thus providing us secondhand witnesses to what Christians originally believed about Jesus. Therefore, we have at least some means of checking the accuracy of Sir Leigh Teabing's revelation that "More than *eighty* gospels were considered for the New Testament, and yet only a relative few were chosen for inclusion— Matthew, Mark, Luke, and John among them" (*The Da Vinci Code,* p. 231). To begin with, Teabing's statement is itself problematic. No other gospels are found in the New Testament, so the canonical Gospels are not "among" any other gospels, unless we consider the epistle to the Hebrews to be some type of rudimentary gospel. So Matthew, Mark, Luke, and John must either be considered to be four among the eighty with the result that seventy-six other gospels exist that we are looking for in our earlier sources—or our New Testament contains other gospels, which is simply not the case.

To trace the existence of earlier texts, we first need to examine what hints remain that would prove the theory that there were other writings outside the New Testament. The earliest quotations of early Christian writings that were not included in the canon are in the New Testament itself. The earliest quotations from and references to lost biblical books are found in Acts and in the epistles of Paul, Peter, and Jude.

Luke, the author of Acts, records a saying of Jesus that is not recorded in any other existing source, a saying that is surprisingly not found in the Gospel Luke wrote. He reports that Jesus said, "It is more blessed to give than to receive" (Acts 20:35), an evidence that this quotation derives from an early source that is now lost to us.

Unlike any other author in the New Testament, Luke wanted everyone to know that he was aware of previous sources and that he freely used them when writing his own account of the life of Jesus: "Forasmuch as many have taken in hand to set forth in order a declaration of those things which are most surely believed among us, Even as they delivered them unto us, which from the beginning were eyewitnesses, and ministers of the word; It seemed good to me also, having had perfect understanding of all things from the very first, to write unto thee" (Luke 1:1–3).

Luke's sources are very early indeed. And he equates them with the eyewitness generation, making them possibly the earliest sources mentioned anywhere in the history of Christianity. Luke then presents his Gospel account of Jesus' life in which Jesus is decidedly divine, the Savior of the world, and more than a mortal man, thus reflecting the stance of those early sources.

If the earliest sources did portray Jesus as merely a mortal man and if later authors altered that belief, then Luke is probably one of the very first to radically alter the earliest sources on Jesus' life, though no evidence exists that he did so.

To confirm that other early sources existed in the decades after Jesus' death, our search for such lost scriptures should be expanded to include Paul. Without doubt, Paul is our earliest writer in the New Testament; and, like Luke, he also knew of sources that were earlier than or at least contemporary to our New Testament Gospels. In probably the earliest New Testament writing,

1 Thessalonians, Paul makes reference to a saying of Jesus that is not found in our Gospels. He reports to the saints in Thessalonica the Lord's saying that "we which are alive and remain unto the coming of the Lord shall not prevent them which are asleep. For the Lord himself shall descend from heaven with a shout, with the voice of the archangel, and with the trump of God: and the dead in Christ shall rise first" (4:15–16).

The exact quotation recalled by Paul is difficult to identify because it appears that he has paraphrased a rather well-known saying of Jesus. Paul certainly heard or read this saying from an earlier source, confirming the existence of earlier sources that have their origins in the first two decades after Jesus' death, prior to Paul writing his epistles. Moreover, Paul's source clearly implies that Jesus was believed to be God because it is He who will return from heaven with a shout and at the sound of the voice of an archangel, both decidedly divine actions.

Other scattered references in Paul's epistles, which can be dated to the period between A.D. 50–65, confirm that he believed Jesus to be divine and that he was familiar with some of the events from the last days of Jesus' life. In fact, we have no hint that Paul's sources, or Luke's for that matter, taught anything other than the divinity of Jesus. For example, Paul records that Jesus was crucified on a cross (see 1 Corinthians 1:23; Philippians 2:8); that He was betrayed on the night He administered the sacrament to the disciples (see 1 Corinthians 11:23–26); that He was resurrected after three days (see 1 Corinthians 15:4); that Paul had seen the resurrected Savior (see 1 Corinthians 15:8; Galatians 1:15–16); that some of the Jews were involved in taking His life under the governor Pontius Pilate (see 1 Corinthians 2:8; 1 Thessalonians 2:14–15; 1 Timothy 6:13); and that Jesus was crucified near the Passover celebration (see 1 Corinthians 5:7).

Although some of these details could be discounted as nothing more than historical footnotes about a supposedly mortal prophet Jesus, some of them clearly teach His divinity—that is, the Resurrection—and they also agree with the accounts in the four Gospels where Jesus is certainly portrayed as a God.

That Paul had access to early sources is undeniable. We have no hint in either Luke's or Paul's writings that their sources presented a different view of Jesus; instead, the most natural conclusion is that those early sources were similar to the accounts presented in Luke and Paul and, by comparison, to the other New Testament Gospels.

Five references to Jesus from first-century and early second-century authors outside the New Testament confirm the belief that the earliest Christians believed Jesus to be divine, even though the writers themselves were not Christians. These authors, whether they had seen Christian texts or learned from practical experience, unanimously confirm that early Christians believed in the divinity of Jesus. These four authors, who are either Roman or Jewish, report:

1. "Now, there was about this time Jesus, a wise man, if it be lawful to call him a man, for he was a doer of wonderful works—a teacher of such men as receive the truth with pleasure. He drew over to him both many of the Jews, and many of the Gentiles. He was [the] Christ; and when Pilate, at the suggestion of the principal men amongst us, had condemned him to the cross, those that loved him at the first did not forsake him, for he appeared to them alive again the third day, as the divine prophets had foretold these and ten thousand other wonderful things concerning him; and the tribe of Christians, so named from him, are not extinct at this day" (Josephus, *Antiquities* 18.3.63–64).[1]

2. "Festus was now dead, and Albinus was but upon the road; so he assembled the sanhedrin of judges, and brought before them the brother of Jesus, who was called Christ" (Josephus, *Antiquities* 20.1.200).[2]

3. "Therefore, to scotch the rumour [of . . .], Nero

substituted as culprits, and punished with the utmost refinements of cruelty, a class of men, loathed for their vices, whom the crowd styled Christians. Christus, the founder of the name, had undergone the death penalty in the reign of Tiberius, by sentence of the procurator Pontius Pilatus" (Tacitus, *Annals* 15.44).[3]

4. "Since the Jews constantly made disturbances at the instigation of Chrestus, he expelled them from Rome" (Suetonius, *Claudius* 25.4).[4]

5. "They [the Christians] were in the habit of meeting on a certain fixed day before it was light, when they sang in alternate verses a hymn to Christ, as to a god, and bound themselves by a solemn oath, not to any wicked deeds, but never to commit any fraud, theft or adultery, never to falsify their word, nor deny a trust when they should be called upon to deliver it up; after which it was their custom to separate, and then reassemble to partake of food—but food of an ordinary and innocent kind" (Pliny, *Epistles* 10.96–97).

A well-meaning Christian scribe probably massaged the first quotation of Josephus, believing that he could enhance Josephus' testimony of Jesus Christ. However, even with the removal of the overtly Christian insertion, a "tribe" of Christians obviously had gathered together in the name of Christ. The final quotation adds that these Christians would often make disturbances over Chrestus, a Latin misspelling of the Greek title *Christ,* indicating that they were passionate about Him and were put in a position where they felt the need to defend Him. Whether these disturbances can be traced to a belief that Jesus was the Messiah cannot be proved, but we would have a difficult time arguing that they preserve evidence of a group of Christians, or anybody else for that matter, who believed in a mortal prophet named Jesus without any overtones of His being divine.

The earliest Christian authors to comment or write about Jesus after the close of the New Testament were Clement of Rome (wrote A.D. 95–96), Ignatius of Antioch (lived A.D. 35–107), the author of the *Didache* (wrote c. A.D. 150), Papias (c. A.D. 70–140), the author of the *Epistle of Barnabas* (c. A.D. 100), Polycarp of Smyrna (wrote A.D. 110), the author of *Hermas* (wrote c. A.D. 100), and the author of *2 Clement* (wrote A.D. 120–170). Each of these Christian authors quotes extensively from the New Testament, and, without equivocation, each of them recognizes the divinity of Jesus, whom they refer to as *Lord, God,* and *Savior.* Additionally, they do not quote extensively from other so-called gospels.

In fact, nowhere can we find any hint that any of them believed Jesus was simply a mortal prophet and nothing more. Moreover, they each quote from various writings of the New Testament and from texts that are now lost, but none of their quotations are from a source that appears to discount the divinity of Jesus in any way. Some of their references to Jesus are illustrative of their belief in Him:

1. "Being especially mindful of the words of the Lord Jesus which He spake, teaching us meekness and long-suffering" (1 Clement 13).[5]

2. "And I know that He was possessed of a body not only in His being born and crucified, but I also know that He was so after His resurrection, and believe that He is so now. When, for instance, He came to those who were with Peter, He said to them, 'Lay hold, handle Me, and see that I am not an incorporeal spirit'" (Iganatius, *Smyrneans,* 3).[6]

3. In the *Epistle of Barnabas,* the author plainly refers to the resurrection of Jesus Christ as well as to the vinegar and gall given to Him while He hung on the cross.

The numbers of these quotations and references could be expanded, but all evidence points to the simple conclusion that the earliest writers considered Jesus to be divine, their resurrected

Lord and their Savior. In fact, we simply have no evidence that any of His followers thought otherwise.

Obviously, non-Christian authors felt differently about the divinity of Jesus, but the question is whether the earliest records preserve any information indicating that *Christians* believed in a prophet named Jesus and also whether later Church leaders suppressed all records containing information indicating such. Importantly, when the earliest sources speak of Jesus or the words of Jesus, they almost universally quote from the writings of the New Testament. That is not to say that some of their quotations do not derive from other sources outside the New Testament, but even those outside sources confirm that they believed in the divinity of Jesus.

To summarize what we know thus far, we can be certain that the earliest sources to mention Jesus or His followers universally confirm the portrait of Him presented in the Gospels and other writings of the New Testament. Jesus was their Lord and Savior, and they felt a great appreciation for His words and teachings.

Other Writings about Jesus

Many have wondered whether other writings existed that preserve different views about Jesus in the first century. The most straightforward answer is that there are numerous writings about Jesus that present a different view of Him and His teachings. Some of these writings have been passed on to us through scribal copying, and others have been discovered through accident or by professional archaeologists. Perhaps among these documents there are even eighty other gospels and thousands of other documents about early Christianity, as Teabing revealed to Sophie Neveu when he said that "thousands of documents already existed [before Constantine] chronicling His life as a *mortal* man" (*The Da Vinci Code,* p. 234).

Some early Christian authors, Peter and Jude for example,

Discoveries from Nag Hammadi, Egypt

Nag Hammadi Codices, c. A.D. 300, Institute for Antiquity and Christianity at Claremont Graduate University, Claremont, California. Discovered near Nag Hammadi in Egypt, these twelve codices (books), and a portion of a thirteenth codex, are one of the most important textual discoveries of the modern era. As church leaders defined the canon in the fourth century, certain books were deemed heretical. The Nag Hammadi codices, shown here in their original leather bindings, preserve the largest single collection of noncanonical Christian texts. *Used by Permission, Institute for Antiquity and Christianity at Claremont Graduate University, Claremont, California*

preserve information about other sources known by early Christian writers. Peter and Jude used noncanonical sources when they wrote their general epistles to the saints, thus demonstrating that they had a larger library of texts they considered helpful and inspirational than we have today. For example, the author of Jude quoted briefly from the apocryphal book *1 Enoch* as well as from the *Testament of Moses* (see Jude 1:9, 14).

Eventually, both of these writings were excluded from the Hebrew canon and then later from the New Testament canon for legitimate concerns over their authorship and antiquity, but portions of both have been preserved. These sources, although they do not mention Jesus or anything concerning Christianity generally, demonstrate that early Christian authors used a more expanded canon than that which has been preserved today. These sources are mostly of Jewish origin, and some show traces of having been altered by Christian scribes.

Of all textual discoveries pertaining to the New Testament, perhaps the most important collection of Christian documents was found in Nag Hammadi, Egypt, in 1945. As we have seen already, the earliest documents do teach the divinity of Jesus, but other books may have presented a different view. Some of these documents will be discussed later.

Moving beyond those books and sources that are explicitly mentioned in our earliest sources—the New Testament writings—we know about literally hundreds of Christian documents from the second century and later. Before we can appreciate whether any of these documents are of comparable value to our New Testament texts, we must first understand the origins of these documents.

Early Christian texts do not record the date when they were composed, nor do they generally record an author's name. Christian tradition has preserved the names associated with each text; and, beginning in the second and third centuries, Christian scribes began to write the authors' names either at the end or the beginning of the books. But, as a general rule, the earliest copies of the New Testament texts are written without title or date. By the time the names of the authors began to be copied with the texts, the dates when the texts had been originally written were already lost.

Today, scholars look for internal and external clues that indicate when a text was written. For example, the Nag Hammadi texts were bound or rebound with a piece of leather that bears a date in the mid-fourth century; therefore, the texts that were found there can be dated prior to that time. Other suggestions for dating can be found internally within the text, which might refer to a datable event or a person whose dates are known. At other times, scholars look for oblique references, such as the Gospel of

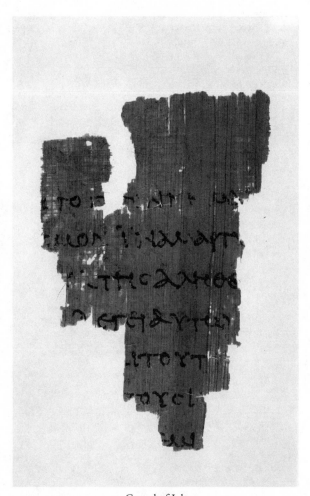

Gospel of John

Manuscript p⁵² (John 19:37–38), A.D. 125, The John Rylands Library, University of Manchester, England. There is universal agreement that this papyrus manuscript dating from the first quarter of the first century is the earliest known fragment of the New Testament. The New Testament, therefore, constitutes the earliest source on the life of Jesus, unlike *The Da Vinci Code*'s unsupported claim that manuscripts from the Dead Sea Scrolls and Nag Hammadi are the earliest. *Reproduced Courtesy of the University Librarian and Director, The John Rylands University Library, University of Manchester (England)*

Nag Hammadi's Text

Gospel of Thomas leaf, c. A.D. 300, Institute for Antiquity and Christianity at Claremont Graduate University, Claremont, California. The most famous of the Nag Hammadi tractates, the *Gospel of Thomas* supposedly records 114 sayings of Jesus. According to the prologue, the resurrected Jesus revealed the sayings to His disciple Didymos Judas Thomas, who should be equated with the Apostle Thomas in the New Testament. Many of the sayings are found in the New Testament Gospels in different forms, a fact that has touched off a series of scholarly debates concerning which account is earlier—the *Gospel of Thomas* or the canonical Gospels. *Used by Permission, Zev Radovan/BibleLandPictures.com*

Matthew's reference to the fall of Jerusalem (which occurred in A.D. 70) in the parable of the vineyard when the vineyard is taken and given to another nation (see Matthew 21:33–43). Needless to say, dating any early text is largely a matter of impression and rarely a matter of direct physical evidence.

These circumstances affect our study of lost scriptures because many scholars have supposed that certain documents are early, such as the *Gospel of Thomas* or the *Gospel of Peter,* whereas other equally prominent scholars reject these early dates. The vast majority of these documents clearly present different forms of Christianity and different beliefs about Jesus—many of them deemed heretical by third- and fourth-century Christian writers. Increasingly, however, scholars are advocating that these documents contain the thoughts and writings of Christians whose divergent views competed with the branch of Christianity that came to dominate all others.

In other words, these divergent texts were not created by Christians who had broken away from the mainstream; instead, they represent very early independent forms of the faith that were eventually suppressed and marginalized. Moreover, these same scholars contend that many of these documents are as early as the writings contained in the New Testament.

Forgoing any further discussion of whether such early dates are warranted, we will instead look at whether these documents present something like that proposed in *The Da Vinci Code,* which reports that prior to the Council of Nicea (A.D. 325), the followers of Jesus viewed Him as a mortal prophet.

A sampling of these documents, focusing particularly on those that have been assigned very early dates, reveals not only that they preserve the belief that Jesus is divine but also, in many cases, that Jesus is spoken of in terms that make Him appear never even to have been mortal. Those who professed such beliefs were called "docetists," and they felt that our four Gospels presented a portrait of Jesus that was *too* mortal.

Here are some of their references to Jesus in their own words. From the *Gospel of Thomas,* a work that some have dated to the period before our canonical Gospels, comes this endorsement of the divinity of Jesus: "Jesus said, 'I am the light that is over all things. I am all: from me all came forth, and to me all attained. Split a piece of wood; I am there. Lift up the stone, and you will find me there'" (*Gospel of Thomas,* 77).[7] From an unnamed early document, we read, "Then said the Savior to him: Woe unto you blind that see not!" (Papyrus Oxyrhynchus, 840).[8] The apocryphal *Gospel of Mary* includes the following statement of Jesus: "When the blessed one [Jesus] had said this, he greeted them all, saying, 'Peace be with you. Receive my peace to yourselves. Beware that no one lead you astray, saying, Lo here! or Lo there!'"[9] The challenge is not in finding references to the divinity of Jesus but rather in finding anything that implies He was *not* divine.

No doubt other gospels and letters written by early Christians have been lost. Explicit mention is made of some of these documents, such as the lost letter to the Corinthian saints (see 1 Corinthians 5:9) and Paul's letter to the Laodiceans (see Colossians 4:16). Some of Luke's sources have also been lost, and many early Christian writers mention other books of scripture that are no longer extant. But the writings that do survive are universal in their presentation of the divinity of Jesus. Whether these documents are rediscovered through archaeology or through continued copying of their texts, they all confirm the fact that the earliest Christians believed Jesus to be their Lord and Savior.

Lost Christian Texts

Among those books that have been lost through suppression, damage, or other means, a potential exists for some of them to present a radically different view of Jesus. Although this outcome remains a theoretical possibility, it simply cannot be confirmed. No early author, Christian or otherwise, hinted that such divergent documents existed in their lifetimes, but the possibility nonetheless remains a theoretical one.

Any scholar can offer a hypothesis concerning the contents of these missing documents, but such a hypothesis cannot be used in any meaningful way to shape our understanding of Jesus and early Christianity. One revealing statement may help underscore the motivations for theorizing that the contents of such lost documents would so radically depart from our earliest sources. In *The Da Vinci Code,* in his somewhat pompous lecture to Sophie, Leigh Teabing states, "The vast majority of *educated* Christians know the history of their faith. Jesus was indeed a great and powerful man" (*The Da Vinci Code,* p. 234; emphasis added). So the real dupes in *The Da Vinci Code* are the millions of unsuspecting Christians who continue to believe that God is real and that Jesus was the Savior of the world. Educated Christians have always known the truth of their faith; they did not need to rediscover this information through documents. Therefore, these lost documents are essentially superfluous, even in *The DaVinci Code.* They are simply secondary confirmations of what educated Christians have known all along.

We cannot help but notice the overt bias in such a conclusion. In the novel, those who believe in Jesus are described as uneducated and having had half-truths foisted upon them unsuspectingly, whereas those who are educated know the reality behind Jesus. Fortunately, modern revelation and prophets, scriptures such as the Book of Mormon, and personal testimony all confirm that Jesus is indeed divine and the Lord of our salvation.

Each generation will continue to propose a scholarly portrait of Jesus, and even some Christians in the first century likely presented such a view. That such a view was proposed or possible in the first century, however, does not make it a reality.

Constantine

The Roman emperor Constantine remains one of the most important figures in Christian history. Known in his lifetime as Gaius Flavius Valerius Aurelius Constantinus and later as Saint Constantine or Constantine the Great, he ruled Rome from A.D. 25 July 306 until his death in A.D. 337. For the most part, he was a capable ruler who ascended to his position as sole ruler of Rome through birth and military success.

Constantine grew up as a typical Roman ruler, worshiping the gods of Rome and offering sacrifice in their temples to gain their favor. According to sources that report his conversion in the way Constantine told the story, the emperor was converted through a remarkable vision. During a battle with the emperor Maxentius at Milvan Bridge north of Rome (A.D. 312), Constantine and his forces were on the verge of collapse. At midday, he had a vision in which he was shown the labarum, which is a sign derived from the two Greek letters *Chi* (X) and *Rho* (R) superimposed on one another. The emperor was told in this vision that he would conquer under this sign, which is itself an acronym meaning "Christ the King" or "Christ Is King," or the first two letters of

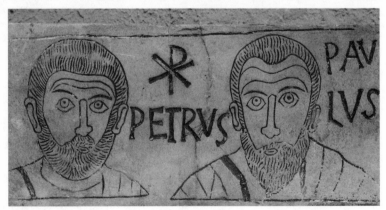

Chi-Rho sign
The Apostles Peter and Paul Relief, c. A.D. 313, Vatican Museum, Vatican State. This relief highlights the monogram of Jesus Christ (Chi-Rho) in the center above Peter's (Petrvs) name. *Used by permission, Erich Lessing/Art Resources, N.Y.*

the name *Christ* in Greek. Following the advice given to him in this vision, Constantine's forces were able to overthrow the forces of Maxentius and obtain sole control of Rome. The vision, however, had an indelible effect on the emperor, who began to dismantle some of the official forms of persecution against Christians.

In the year following the battle at Milvan Bridge, Constantine issued the Edict of Milan (A.D. 313), which declared Roman neutrality with regard to religious worship and ended any official government-sanctioned persecution of Christians. The edict made it possible for Christians to own land and hold public office. The edict also returned property to the Christians, such as buildings that had been confiscated and sold during the third-century persecutions under Diocletian. In an effort to set things right with his Christian constituents, Constantine began building churches in the Holy Land. Constantine, however, was not solely responsible for issuing the edict, which was given under the names of two of the Roman rulers—Constantine and Licinius, the eastern emperor.

Constantine and Licinius may have been following in the footsteps of their predecessor Galerius, who issued an edict of toleration from Nicomedia in A.D. 311. Unlike the edict of Galerius, which granted a temporary indulgence to Christians for not having sacrificed to the gods of the state, the Edict of Milan permanently removed the requirement that Christians take part in the civic cult.

The wording of Galerius's edict may reveal some of Constantine's motivation for becoming a Christian. The Romans, like the Greeks, believed that civic well-being was maintained through proper worship of the gods. They believed that their temples and shrines needed to be properly maintained and cared for and that neglect would ultimately result in punishment and retribution. Christians, however, had consistently refused to take part in the civic cults. They would not make sacrifices to Greek or Roman deities, nor would they participate in the worship of the emperor, behaviors that were interpreted by the government as hostile acts against the state.

When the Roman army suffered defeat or the economy struggled, the Christians were blamed for invoking the wrath of the gods. When Galerius issued his edict of toleration, he asked that the Christians be given an indulgence for not praying for the public safety, but his edict also encouraged them to do so in the future.

Constantine and Licinius's later edict may have been aimed at procuring a similar result through a different means. At the turn of the fourth century, the Roman emperors obviously had realized that the numbers of Christians throughout the empire were significant and that it was politically advantageous to bring them into the civic mainstream. Galerius offered an invitation to enter the public mainstream without any punishment for previous actions. However, not only did Constantine issue an invitation but also his vision was promoted as an act of welcome and a personal embracing of the faith. Not only did the new emperor tolerate the faith of Christians but also he personally accepted their ideals and beliefs.

Events in the eastern empire, however, reveal that Constantine's actions were interpreted politically. The Sassanid rulers of Persia began persecuting Christians almost immediately because the Christians in their empires were now viewed as allies of Rome. There is even an apocryphal letter wherein Constantine supposedly asked the Persian leader Shapur II to protect Christians in his empire in c. A.D. 324.

Similarly, in A.D. 320, the eastern emperor Licinius revolted against Constantine and took direct aim against their edict of toleration. Surprisingly, Licinius's own wife was Christian, but he felt he could unify the empire under the banner of paganism rather than Christianity. Constantine, who had realized the political expediency of befriending the Christians, was now challenged on this very point by his brother-in-law, who obviously felt that pagans were still the dominant subculture. During the civil war that ensued, Constantine defeated his brother-in-law, thus proving that Christians represented a significant portion of the populace. Both sides interpreted the civil war as a battle of religions, paganism against Christianity, Old Rome against New Rome; and much as he had done at the battle at Milvan Bridge, Constantine conquered under the sign of the Lord Jesus Christ. An important political ally was also made during the battle, as the French openly supported Constantine.

Was Constantine's Conversion Genuine?

One of the most important places to look to discover whether Constantine's conversion was genuine is in his later life, after he had issued the Edict of Milan (A.D. 313) and ascended as sole ruler of the Roman Empire (A.D. 324). What historians have long noticed is that the emperor continued to use the iconography of paganism in coins and inscriptions. It is as if he continued to be pagan *and* Christian, which is surprising by modern standards but would have been expected by ancient standards.

The Roman emperor was the head of the civic cult and was often portrayed as the *pontifex maximus,* or "high priest," on coins. Even though Constantine had converted to Christianity, he was still the emperor and leader in civic affairs, which meant that he would continue to preside over certain pagan religious activities. His conversion did not remove his responsibilities as the *pontifex maximus;* instead, he maintained a leadership position for the civic cult, a stance that he likewise adopted for Christianity. He was the head of the state and the head of the Church, and it would have been remarkable for any emperor to undergo a conversion process whereby he became subservient to a priest or any other religious leader. Certainly he knew of the role of bishops in the Church, but his position as emperor surpassed theirs, even though they better understood the workings of the Church.

Other examples show Constantine's dual identity as civic leader *and* converted Christian. In coins stamped during the latter part of Constantine's reign, the emperor is depicted as the sun god *Sol Invictus,* or the "unconquerable sun." Other images show the emperor with the labarum, the acronym for "Christ Is King," on his shield or helmet. Even later images show the emperor in an idealized representation where he appears as a deity. This amalgamation of pagan and Christian symbols could be interpreted as an intentional stratagem to bring adherents of these disparate religious movements together, but it was also an outgrowth of the emperor's civic duties.

Whether Constantine was intentionally trying to dominate his political opponents through religious unification is doubtful, but he was also not ignorant of the great benefit that would befall him if his constituents were united. In his later life, he sought to unify the disparate Christian factions within the Empire and actually delivered public sermons in Rome on Christian topics.

At the time of Constantine, the Church was divided over issues of authority, practice, doctrine, and scripture. We are correct to recognize that some Christians accepted a twenty-seven-book canon of the New Testament, whereas others accepted such apocryphal works as the Acts of Paul, the *Epistle of Barnabas,* or the *Shepherd of Hermas.* Christians from all over the Empire had accepted some of these books as scripture for decades, and they held to them as tenaciously as they did the four canonical Gospels and the letters of Paul, Peter, James, John, and Jude.

These same Christians were also divided over the issue of how much central authority the bishops should be given and whether such a thing as a Church-wide leader existed. Issues of doctrine were probably the most divisive, with the predominant concern being whether the Son of God was a created being (a belief known as Arianism) or whether He existed from all eternity to all eternity. This schism threatened to tear the Church apart.

Constantine, who realized that such regional infighting over doctrine and texts would eventually rupture the Church and cause fallout among the citizens of the Empire, convened a council to settle the issue. He had no authority in the Church to convene such a gathering of local church leaders, but interestingly no bishops claimed to have such Church-wide authority either. Constantine called the council together because he was the emperor, but the meeting was turned over to the bishops, who were given an opportunity to settle some of the issues facing their congregations. The council, known today as the Council of Nicea (A.D. 325), was patterned after the Church-wide council held in Acts 15 where some of the leading brethren—Peter, James, Paul, and Barnabas—met to discuss the issue of circumcision.

Constantine's exact role in the conference is unclear, and he apparently neither directed the conversations nor stipulated the conclusions that the participants should reach. Among other things, the council decided that the views of Arius and his followers were heretical and should be rejected outright. Arian bishops were compelled to renounce their heretical beliefs and bring their views into harmony with the Church. With sufficient spin, the denunciation of Arius and his beliefs could be interpreted as a vote on the humanity of Jesus because the central issue of Arianism was whether Jesus was a created being. Arius did not stipulate that Jesus had been created during birth here on earth but only asked the question whether there ever was a time when Jesus did not exist.

The Arian faction narrowly lost, but some have confused this vote with the issue of Jesus' humanity when, in reality, both Arius and orthodox Christians unanimously believed in the divinity of

Jesus. Constantine appears to have had little concern over whether the Arians or orthodox Christians prevailed. Later in his life, he was baptized by a bishop with Arian sympathies, even after those beliefs had been denounced at the Council of Nicea.

Although not directly related to the central issue of the Council of Nicea, Constantine also commissioned the copying of fifty Bibles on parchment to be used in the churches throughout the Empire. This occurred because, during the decades prior to Constantine's reign, Christianity had been vigorously suppressed in an empire-wide persecution under Diocletian (A.D. 284–305). Diocletian had ordered that churches be confiscated and sold and that all Christian books should be publicly burned. This empire-wide persecution drastically reduced the number of copies of the scriptures available to local congregations. And when Christianity was no longer suppressed under Constantine, the need arose to make copies of the Bible readily and quickly available.

Some of the actual copies made under Constantine's edict may have survived. The *Codex Sinaiticus* is likely one of the copies of the Bible that Constantine commissioned. What is unfortunate is that Constantine's commission to make copies of the Bible has been taken out of context and has been used to infer that he was responsible for creating the Bible. He certainly contributed in a major way in preserving the text of the Bible, but he did not *create* the Bible. The texts of the Bible before Constantine's edict are nearly identical to the texts that were copied after his edict. In fact, if we use a modern English translation of the Bible, it would be nearly impossible for most readers to distinguish a pre-Constantinian text from a post-Constantinian text. Only minor variations in wording are found, and no variations for the books of the New Testament are found. It is, therefore, misleading to claim that Constantine

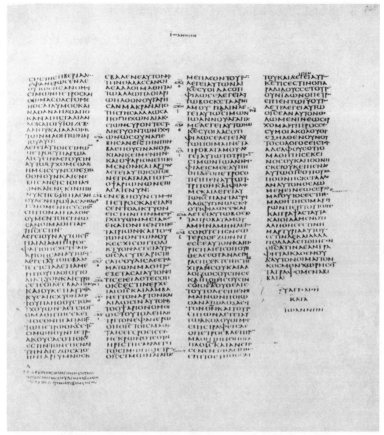

Codex Sinaiticus

Codex Sinaiticus, Greek Bible, fourth century A.D., British Museum, London, England. Discovered in St. Catherine's Monastery in Egypt, this leaf from an early Christian codex may be from one of the copies of the Bible commissioned by the Roman emperor Constantine. *Used by Permission, HIP/Art Resource,* NY

"omitted those gospels that spoke of Christ's *human* traits and embellished those gospels that made Him godlike" (*The Da Vinci Code,* p. 234). Instead, Constantine should be thanked for funding a tremendous effort to make new copies of the New Testament that would be distributed throughout the Empire and for beginning the process that would result in the fixation of the text that began to occur in the fourth century.

The Dead Sea Scrolls and the Nag Hammadi Texts

In 1947, a Bedouin shepherd discovered a cave near the Dead Sea containing ancient Jewish scrolls. Over the course of the next nine years, ten more caves were discovered containing scrolls. By the time the final cave was discovered, the scrolls had already been widely touted as one of the most important discoveries of the modern era. Among the scrolls were copies of every book of the Old Testament, with the exception of Esther, and other writings about community standards, practices, and beliefs. Perhaps the greatest contribution of the scrolls was that they contained the oldest complete copies of the books of the Old Testament known to exist. Essentially, the scrolls provided proof of the accuracy, or inaccuracy in some cases, of the Old Testament text.

Qumran Cave 4

Beginning in 1947, eleven caves in the Judean wilderness were found to contain more than one thousand manuscripts, now known as the Dead Sea Scrolls. Cave 4, pictured here, is among the most famous of these caves, located on the northwestern shore of the Dead Sea. *The Da Vinci Code* claims that the scrolls constitute some of the earliest Christian documents. However, virtually all scholars, including Latterday Saints with access to the documents themselves, universally agree that the library belonged to a group of Jews with absolutely no Christian connections. *Used by Permission, Zev Radovan/BibleLandPictures.com*

The exact reasons why the scrolls were hidden in jars and placed in caves is not entirely certain, although most scholars believe they were placed there to preserve them during the First Jewish War against the Romans (A.D. 66–74). As the legions of Rome moved to reassert their authority in Judea, the community that produced or copied the scrolls hid them away for safekeeping. As far as our knowledge permits us to say, the community that produced the scrolls had no ties to Christianity whatsoever. Instead, the authors and copyists of the scrolls were separatist Jews, who felt that the mainstream forms of their ancestral faith— Pharisees and Sadducees—had gone astray. Some of the writings found in the caves near the Dead Sea are highly critical of the Jewish leadership around the time of Jesus.

Scholars, however, universally recognize that the Dead Sea Scrolls contain no information about Jesus or Christianity. They do contain a wealth of information about Judea and Jerusalem at the time of Jesus, but there is no evidence that any of the texts from the Dead Sea Scrolls discovery make even an oblique reference to Jesus of Nazareth or to any of His disciples. In no way can these scrolls be used to authenticate the text of the New Testament. They do provide a witness to the text of the Bible prior to Constantine, but that text is exclusively the Old Testament, a text that was already well established by the fourth century A.D. when Constantine commissioned fifty copies of the Bible.

Similarly, the Nag Hammadi documents discovered in Egypt provide little evidence for the text of the New Testament prior to Constantine. In 1945, a young boy stumbled upon an ancient Christian library that had probably been hidden by monks in the fourth or fifth century. In all, the boy found twelve books and several loose leaves belonging to a thirteenth book. The books contained apocryphal writings from the New Testament era. Six of the documents were already known prior to the discovery. In all, the discovery yielded thirty new documents that detailed the beliefs of Gnostic Christians in Egypt.

All the documents are written in Coptic, but many of them were originally written in Greek and then translated. Some of the documents are not Christian, such as the copy of Plato's *Republic,* whereas others are only marginally Christian. Perhaps the largest single grouping of documents to be found at Nag Hammadi are the Valentinian treatises that purportedly preserve the writings of the Gnostic teacher Valentinus (c. A.D. 150) and his pupils. These works preserve clear evidence of how Gnostics incorporated philosophical speculation into their Christian beliefs. Jesus, instead of being simply human, in many of the Nag Hammadi texts is actually an angelic mediator figure who teaches mankind the hidden wisdom of the eternities. Jesus is certainly not human in the Nag Hammadi texts, but He is also not the Savior of the world in them. The documents are, in fact, so diverse that they cannot adequately be described as a single genre.

In all probability, the documents were hidden away in the late fourth century as the Christian canon became more clearly and definitively established. The matter of which books should be included in the New Testament canon appears to have become a subject of great interest at the beginning of the fourth century. Paul's letters had received universal recognition as canonical documents, as had the four Gospels now contained in our New Testament. Several canon lists from the third and fourth centuries survive, documenting the process by which our New Testament documents were accepted and placed in their current order. The definitive statement on the canon was made in A.D. 367 in Athanasius's thirty-ninth Festal Letter where he determined the date of the Easter celebration as well as set forth a list of all canonical books in order. That list is exactly like that of our modern New Testament, both in content and in order.

The Dead Sea Scrolls and the Nag Hammadi tractates are of

immeasurable value for the study of first-century Judea and early Christian heresies. The Dead Sea Scrolls preserve documents from some of Jesus' more radical contemporaries and therefore reveal how others reacted to the Jewish hierarchy. In the same vein, the Nag Hammadi tractates preserve the words of Christians who were considered to be heretics. For centuries, scholars have had to rely on secondary sources to understand these early Christian communities. However, for the first time, we have a considerable amount of material written by them expressing their thoughts in their own terms. Some of these documents may even have some early material in them, but none of them rivals the historical value of the four canonical Gospels or the Pauline epistles.

The Nag Hammadi codices are clearly secondary sources, and even scholars who have suggested they are early recognize that much of what they contain is quite late with only traces of early material.

Conclusion

Without doubt, the Bible has had a long and tumultuous history, especially the New Testament. Some books were excluded for obvious reasons, and fortunately the vast majority of those books that were excluded have survived and are still available for study. They were often excluded because of concerns over their authorship, whereas others were excluded because of the strange doctrines and practices they contained. We need to read for only a few moments in some of these documents to realize how different they are from the books of the New Testament.

Theories may abound about what any lost documents contained, although no physical or literary evidence exists that would identify their contents. They may have taught that Jesus was merely human, but even so, the fact that a person may have held that opinion in the first century does not make it true, either then or now. Jesus' earliest followers unanimously believed He was divine. He was their Lord and Savior. Even heretical Christian believers agreed that He was more than a mortal.

Constantine, whether intentionally or not, unified the Christian Church by bringing the disparate parties of the fourth century into greater doctrinal harmony. He did not settle all of their disputes, but he certainly began the process that would yield a more centralized leadership in the postpersecution environment of the fourth century. He paid for numerous copies of the Bible to be made, and he returned church property to its rightful owners. He began the process that would make it popular and acceptable to be Christian. For all of those things, he should be thanked.

And whether such fantastic finds as that purportedly discovered by the Knights Templar underneath ruins of the Jerusalem Temple Mount will ever come to light remains to be seen. According to *The Da Vinci Code,* the knights dug for ten years through solid rock to discover these documents, but we have to wonder why they simply did not look for the original door through which the documents were taken and placed there in the first place. As with so many stories about the Bible, it is often easier to believe that someone excavating solid rock for ten years could discover something more profound than that which was readily apparent from the start.

CHAPTER 3

A Married Savior?

"As I said earlier, the marriage of Jesus and
Mary Magdalene is part of the historical record."

(*The Da Vinci Code,* p. 245)

The allegedly unquestionable marriage of Jesus and Mary
Magdalene is one of the pivots on which the plot of *The Da Vinci
Code* turns. Main characters of the novel introduce this concept
with certitude. Not only does the character named Leigh Teabing
declare the marriage to be part of the historical record but Robert
Langdon also chimes in that "Jesus was a Jew . . . and the social
decorum during that time virtually forbid a Jewish man to be
unmarried. According to Jewish custom, celibacy was condemned,
and the obligation for a Jewish father was to find a suitable wife
for his son. If Jesus were not married, at least one of the Bible's
gospels would have mentioned it and offered some explanation for
His unnatural state of bachelorhood" (*The Da Vinci Code,* p. 245).

Such propositions beg for a response *regardless* of one's religious affiliation. But they are of special interest to Latter-day
Saints because of the exalted and exalting status of marriage in our
theology; however, an even more significant doctrinal issue is at
stake. Ultimately, the novel falsely argues that if Jesus were married and fathered a child, then He would be human and not
divine. Also, the book incorrectly argues that the earliest unaltered

gospels support both the proposition that Jesus was married and that He was not divine. Leigh Teabing asserts that "a child of Jesus would undermine the critical notion of Christ's divinity and therefore the Christian Church" (*The Da Vinci Code,* p. 254).

Whether Jesus was married is not as important a question as this last conclusion. Even those scholars who have argued that Jesus was most likely not married have consistently noted that if Jesus were married or had children, such a circumstance does not undermine His divinity or the power of His atoning sacrifice. Celibacy was never a requirement for divinity. Because Jesus believed the family relationship was part of God's plan (see Mark 10:9), including well-loved and nurtured children (see Mark 10:13–16), we have no reason to believe that Jesus thought marriage was defiling or that normal marriage relations were unholy. In the end, *The Da Vinci Code*'s argument is no argument at all.

This reasoning leaves us with the question about what the historical sources tell us of Jesus, of marriage, and of Mary Magdalene. The fact is that the canonical New Testament, our earliest and most reliable source for the life and ministry of Jesus Christ, does not provide us all the information we would like to know about Him.

It is virtually silent on the period from His birth to the beginning of His ministry. It includes, of course, a brief discussion of His life when, as a twelve-year-old boy, Jesus accompanied His mother and Joseph to Jerusalem for the feast of Passover (see Luke 2:40–52). Otherwise, we find no information in the four Gospels about the first thirty years of Jesus' life, so any argument about His life during this period is an argument from silence—the weakest kind of argument. But what about other sources?

Restoration Scriptures

Nothing in Restoration scriptures explicitly states that Jesus was married. On the other hand, neither do Restoration scriptures contain any statement indicating He was not married. The scriptures simply are silent regarding any explicit mention of marriage involving Jesus of Nazareth and any woman. Like the New Testament record, the focus and intent of Restoration scriptures are to point us to Jesus as the Christ and to testify of His atoning sacrifice, gospel plan, mission, relationship to His disciples, His Church, and the worlds He created—all of which He redeemed through an infinite and eternal sacrifice (see Doctrine and Covenants 76:22–24; 41–42).

It is in this context, rather than one of personal circumstance, that Jesus described Himself as the Bridegroom. The Church is His bride, meaning that His whole focus and fidelity were centered on the eternal happiness of the bride—the members of His Church collectively and all of His Father's children. As the Bridegroom, He would be taken away from the bride to offer Himself as a sacrifice for her, to atone for her sins as well as the sins of the whole world (see Matthew 9:15; Mark 2:19–20). Jesus gave the parable of the Ten Virgins to teach His disciples that they—the bride—must be loyal to Him and prepare purposefully for the return of the Bridegroom (see Matthew 25:1–13).

Significantly, Jesus continued the metaphor of marriage in this dispensation to teach us that preparation for the Second Coming requires absolute faithfulness and fidelity to Him and His gospel—the kind of loyalty demanded of marriage partners to one another (see Doctrine and Covenants 33:17–18; 88:92; 133:10, 19). The canonized Gospels are also concerned only with this aspect of Jesus' "marriage." Any discussion of the matter of marriage in Jesus' personal life immediately takes our focus away from the central, critical core message of salvation that comes "only in and through the name of Christ, the Lord Omnipotent" (Mosiah 3:17).

In a sense, those who argue vigorously for or against a married Jesus do us a disservice by deflecting our attention away from *the* very thing that matters most. And the thing that matters most—the most important event in time or all eternity—is the Atonement, including the Resurrection, of Jesus Christ. *The Da Vinci Code* does not have as one of its objectives the strengthening of readers' faith in the divinity of Jesus Christ (Jesus as God) or the infinite, eternal, incomparable ramifications of His redemptive act. The novel does have the effect, through misstatement and innuendo, of getting people to argue over such questions as whether Jesus was married. When *The Da Vinci Code* is regarded as anything more than fiction, it changes the discussion—and not for the better. When it states categorically that Jesus was married, it also claims that the Roman Catholic Church covered up the facts about that marriage to protect the divinity of a very human Jesus.

Inference from Scripture

The Da Vinci Code argues that if Jesus were not married, one of the Gospels would have noted this anomaly and offered an explanation for it. Maybe, maybe not. This same kind of reasoning is actually used by those who argue vociferously for an unmarried Jesus. They say that there is no mention of Jesus' wife in the New Testament. Whenever Jesus' family is referred to, it is His mother, brothers, and sisters who are mentioned—but never a wife. There is no mention of His being widowed. Moreover, the wives of Jesus' apostles, the brothers of the Lord, and Cephas (Peter) *are* mentioned (see 1 Corinthians 9:5)—but not the wife of Jesus. This shows, the argument goes, that the early Church was not embarrassed by or averse to talking about the wives of its leaders. Therefore, the argument concludes, because Jesus' wife is never mentioned, He must not have been married.

Again, maybe, maybe not. The number of times wives are mentioned explicitly or by inference in the entire New Testament is very small, and such mention is always in the context of some other point—made in passing, as it were. Just because something is not mentioned does not mean it did not exist. We come back to the point made earlier that arguments from silence are the weakest kind, as the various proponents of opposing viewpoints regarding Jesus' marriage so eloquently demonstrate.

Factually, it is simply too sweeping to say, as *The Da Vinci Code* does, that it was un-Jewish to be unmarried in the first century A.D. Paul was likely unmarried during his missionary journeys, and his countrymen still regarded him as being Jewish. This point is evident in the account of his arrest. Certain Asian Jews thought Paul had taken Gentiles into the forbidden precincts of the Jerusalem Temple while undergoing a Jewish purification ceremony (see Acts 21:20–29). By comparison, John the Baptist also appears to be unmarried in the Gospel accounts, yet like Jesus', his marital status is not an integral part of his story or his ministry and therefore is unmentioned. But no one questions John's "Jewishness."

Other historical documents and nonbiblical texts describe Jews who were unmarried. The first-century Jewish historian Josephus, for example, describes the celibate practices of a Jewish group known as the Essenes—a fourth philosophical sect of the Jews, as Josephus calls them (see *Antiquities* 18:1:1, 6; *Jewish War* 2:8:2). But here, we are not equating Jesus with the Essenes.

It is true that first-century Jewish men regarded marriage as an obligation. Genesis 1:28 reports God's command to men and women to be fruitful and fill the earth with posterity. But there were exceptions to the general rule and expectation. So it seems not only inaccurate but also unproductive to argue for Jesus being married on the basis of cultural mores that were not always strictly adhered to.

Other evidence cited from the New Testament in support of Jesus' marriage to Mary Magdalene is really also by inference. In the very sobering and personal matter of Jesus' crucifixion, it is sometimes pointed out that in the Gospel of John, Mary Magdalene does not view the Crucifixion from afar but is found standing right by the Cross with other members of Jesus' family— His mother, His aunt, and John the Beloved, all of whom enjoyed a close personal relationship with Jesus (see John 19:25). Hence, the inference is that Mary Magdalene was probably a family member or close friend, too, and the only reasonable possibility in terms of the family relationship was as a wife. But that is the point—it is only an inference.

More importantly, it is Mary Magdalene, who again, according to John, comes to the tomb of Jesus alone—not with the group of women as in the other synoptic Gospels. She is the first recorded person in history to encounter the risen Lord. Jesus addresses her as "woman," which is translated from the Greek *gynai,* a word that Jesus also uses when speaking to His mother (see John 2:4). This usage certainly can mean "wife" in some contexts, though it more naturally means "woman" (see John 20:13–15). Unfortunately, some ambiguity is preserved because of these two valid translations of the word. In support of the translation "woman," we note that Mary does not immediately seem to understand the word as "wife" when Jesus first addresses her at the tomb. Perhaps Jesus' injunction to Mary to "touch me not" could be interpreted as a reference to a more intimate relationship (see John 20:17). The Greek phrase from which the English is derived, *me mou haptou,* is best rendered as "do not cling to me," "do not keep touching me," and is more suggestive of a more intimate relationship than what we would expect between Jesus and His disciples. But, again, this is inference.

Mary Magdalene may have been among the group of women meeting in the "upper room" after the Savior's ascension, along with the Apostles as described in Acts 1:13–14. The plural of the Greek *gynai,* translated again as "women," could be interpreted as "wives," but the women are not linked specifically to any of the men present. Again, the New Testament data are not specific enough to be of help in concretely discerning the matter of Jesus' purported marriage.

Finally, some have argued that Jesus knows all things, that He "descended below all things" (Doctrine and Covenants 88:6; see also 122:8), and that these aspects of His divinity would not be possible if He were unmarried. However, the same argument could be made regarding, say, sin generally. But it is certain that Jesus never sinned in order to understand it or descend below it.

Nonscriptural Evidence

Is the marriage of Jesus to Mary Magdalene clearly part of the non-New Testament historical record? No, again we know nothing with certainty concerning Jesus' marital status. Statements such as those made in *The Da Vinci Code* are highly interpretive. To support such statements by arguing that if Jesus had been a bachelor, one of the Gospels surely would have mentioned it is, again, an argument from silence—the weakest kind. Therefore, let us look briefly at the nonscriptural historical records to evaluate the validity of the claims put forward in *The Da Vinci Code.*

The main evidence offered by *The Da Vinci Code* for Jesus and Mary Magdalene being married is a text that comes from an extrabiblical corpus of documents known as Gnostic texts. The term *Gnostic* derives from the Greek word *gnosis,* which means "knowledge." In this context, *Gnostic* refers to special knowledge available only to insiders—divine mysteries revealed only to those who are capable and worthy of receiving and understanding this higher-level teaching. The largest modern cache of these Gnostic texts was discovered at Nag Hammadi, Egypt, in the mid-twentieth century. Hence, they are referred to as the Nag Hammadi codices. They purport to be long-lost or secretly held New Testament-like documents, disclosing information that was either unknown, too esoteric for, or even suppressed by early

Nag Hammadi Text

Gospel of Philip, c. A.D. 300, Institute for Antiquity and Christianity at Claremont Graduate University, Claremont, California. Discovered in codex 2 of the Nag Hammadi tractates, the *Gospel of Philip* purports to be a collection of reminiscences of the Apostle Philip. Written c. A.D. 300, the text has no direct connection with Jesus' Apostle of the same name. Unlike our canonical Gospels, the *Gospel of Philip* contains a disjointed series of sayings and deeds of Jesus with little or no narrative framework to place them in their historical context. *Used by Permission, Institute for Antiquity and Christianity at Claremont Graduate University, Claremont, California*

Christianity. They bear such titles as the *Gospel of Thomas, Gospel of Philip, Gospel of Mary, Wisdom of Jesus,* and so on. These documents are of relatively late date or questionable origin and were not included in the New Testament canon or authorized collection of books in our present New Testament.

In *The Da Vinci Code,* the character Leigh Teabing points out a passage from the *Gospel of Philip* as a good place for others to start when looking for historical verification of Jesus' marriage. But even the way this text is introduced through Teabing's dialogue is fraught with inaccuracies. Teabing describes "the Nag Hammadi and Dead Sea scrolls" as the "earliest Christian records" (*The Da Vinci Code,* p. 245). Generally speaking, the Nag Hammadi texts are late—later than the canonical Gospels in our New Testament; and the Dead Sea Scrolls are Jewish texts, not Christian in origin! So much for contextual accuracy.

More problematic still is the way *Gospel of Philip* 63:33–36 is cited in *The Da Vinci Code.* The original passage has its problems: literal gaps in the preserved sentences as well as scholars not being unequivocally sure of the meaning and implication of the wording. These are issues not noted in *The Da Vinci Code* because such problems make statements about the certainty of Jesus' marriage much more tenuous.

The passage, read by the character named Sophie, is printed in the novel as follows: *"And the companion of the Saviour is Mary Magdalene. Christ loved her more than all the disciples and used to kiss her often on her mouth. The rest of the disciples were offended by it and expressed disapproval. They said to him, 'Why do you love her more than all of us?'"* (*The Da Vinci Code,* p. 246). After Sophie finishes reading it, we are told that she is surprised over the words, but she comments out loud that the text "says nothing of marriage" (*The Da Vinci Code,* p. 246). To that, Teabing replies, "*Au contraire.* . . . As any Aramaic scholar will tell you, the word *companion,* in those days, literally meant *spouse*" (*The Da Vinci Code,* p. 246).

In truth, *Gospel of Philip* 63:33–36 is damaged in several places and does not read as smoothly as we are led to believe. Translators have supplied missing words in between the damaged parts of the manuscript by calculating how many letters fit in the gaps and then surmising what words can fit the context of the passage. (Scholars use brackets in their translations to indicate unintended breaks in a text.) In other words, the supplied words are also a product of inference. *Gospel of Philip* 63:33–36, as it is available to us, actually reads: "And the companion of the [Savior is] Mary Magdalene. [But Christ loved] her more than [all] the disciples [and used to] kiss her [often] on her [mouth]. The rest of [the disciples were offended] by it [and expressed disapproval]. They said to him, 'Why do you love her more than all of us?'"[1]

Some authorities inform us that this kind of reconstruction takes great skill, and the challenge with a text like this one is to choose the best options for restoring the damaged portions.

Other scholars have suggested that if we read the sentences that appear just after the telltale "kissing" passage, it begins to appear as though Mary is being associated with the anciently personified concept of Wisdom and that this passage was intended to carry more of the sense of a symbolic, spiritual relationship than a literal, physical one. The full context of the passage then reads: "And the companion of the [Savior is] Mary Magdalene. [But Christ loved] her more than [all] the disciples [and used to] kiss her [often] on her [mouth]. The rest of [the disciples were offended] by it [and expressed disapproval]. They said to him, 'Why do you love her more than all of us?' The Savior answered and said to them, 'Why do I not love you like her?' When a blind man and one who sees are both together in darkness, they are no different from one another. When the light comes, then he who sees will see the light, and he who is blind will remain in darkness."[2]

Embedded in the full context of this passage are some of the Gnostic overtones and undercurrents we expect from this genre of literature. Jesus loves Mary differently (note here He does not say He loves her "more," as the disciples accuse Him of doing) because she sees things differently than other disciples. She has seen with greater light and clarity; she is not blind, not remaining in darkness.

Regarding the commentary proffered by the character Teabing in *The Da Vinci Code*—namely, that "any Aramaic scholar" will tell us that the word *companion* literally meant "spouse"—there is confusion at best and misinformation at worst. First, the *Gospel of Philip* was translated from Greek into Coptic,[3] so an Aramaic scholar would not be the person we would want to consult on matters relating to this Coptic text. Aramaic is a completely different language. The second issue, the literal meaning of the word *companion,* is also not well understood by the literary character or the author of *The Da Vinci Code.* The term in question is a Greek loan-word *Koinonos,* and it can mean "companion," "wife," or "sister" in a spiritual sense. It does not *have* to mean "wife."

Certainly, under normal circumstances, these would not be matters for bona fide scholars to quibble over in a work of fiction. Fiction, by definition, is imaginary. But *The Da Vinci Code* raises the stakes when it presents its concepts as completely accurate fact—and with such pedantic certitude. As already noted elsewhere, on a "fact page" inserted in front of the beginning of the novel, the author of *The Da Vinci Code* declares, "All descriptions of artwork, architecture, documents, and secret rituals in this novel are accurate" (*The Da Vinci Code,* p. 1). The case for Jesus' marriage to Mary Magdalene as put forth in *The Da Vinci Code* is not certain, nor is it a matter of "the historical record" as the novel declares. The *Gospel of Philip* is neither a history of Jesus nor a canonical gospel but is a late pseudepigraphical composition (written by one person but labeled as being authored by an earlier authority—in this case the Apostle Philip) with a theological purpose. Scholars put its date of composition in the second half of the third century A.D. in Syria.[4]

Generally, those documents whose dates of composition are closer to actual events described therein are given greater weight or credence by scholars and historians. The four canonical Gospels were composed earlier than the Gnostic texts. Relying on Joseph Smith's keen prophetic eye and perspective, Latter-day Saints know that the four canonical Gospels are of far greater worth than apocryphal or pseudepigraphical writings (see Doctrine and Covenants 91; JST New Testament). The Prophet indicated that the four Gospels are not histories or literary compositions. They are testimonies!

Latter-day Statements on Jesus' Marriage

Having described why we should not rely on *The Da Vinci Code* for our doctrinal or historical understanding, we turn now to unique evidence supporting the idea that Jesus was married. It should be treated with sensitivity and reverence by Latter-day Saints because, first of all, marriage is a very personal matter and we are discussing here the sacred life of the Son of God. How many of us would be offended if people went around poking into, indeed seeming to crave, the details of our private lives? Secondly, marriage is bound up with our most sacred ordinances and is at the heart of the very reason we came to this earth—to participate in marriage and family life (see Doctrine and Covenants 2:1–3; 49:15–17). Marriage does not seem to be treated with much respect in certain quarters these days. *The Da Vinci Code* and similar discussions do not undertake this issue for any reason other than to diminish the divinity of Christ and reduce everything to base physicality. The discussion in *The Da Vinci Code* strikes one as a kind of historical and spiritual voyeurism. We must be better than that.

Many LDS Church leaders, beginning with the Prophet Joseph Smith, have inferred or believed that Jesus was married. From the Prophet's teachings about Jesus as an example, some Latter-day Saints have concluded that Jesus was married because marriage is an important part of our eternal progression. President Joseph F. Smith taught this concept, indicating that the Lord fulfilled the entire law of God and asked men and women to follow Him.[5]

Other Church leaders also believed that Jesus was married, including Orson Hyde and Wilford Woodruff.[6] There have been, of course, leaders who have been cautious in their observations about the subject, including an important editorial published in the Church's official magazine, the *Improvement Era,* in 1912, indicating that the Church had no official position on the subject of Jesus' own marriage.[7] In recent years, we have, in fact, been counseled by current Prophets and Apostles, such as Elder Joseph B. Wirthlin, that where the scriptures are silent, we should pass over them with reverence and focus on those doctrines that are revealed with clarity.[8]

Conclusion

Countless millions of people are learning about early Christian history, practices, and beliefs through *The Da Vinci Code.* The problem is that the novel often gets it wrong, both in terms of the facts and their interpretation.

The provocative and sensational claim about Jesus' relationship to Mary Magdalene is one example of the novel's unsupportable conclusions.

The New Testament teaches, and most Christians accept, that Jesus was both the divine Son of God and was born of a mortal mother. Nothing in the New Testament or in Restoration scriptures would support the novel's wild claim that "a child of Jesus would undermine the critical notion of Christ's divinity and there-fore the Christian Church" (*The Da Vinci Code,* p. 254).

We, along with other thoughtful and believing New Testament scholars, know of no doctrinal reason why Jesus could not have been married and still be the divine Son of God, capable of and willing to atone for the sins of the world.

On the issue of what the historical record tells us about the subject, we admit that the New Testament record is virtually silent on the marital status of both Jesus and Mary Magdalene.

Restoration scripture provides little additional information on this subject. However, we are left with little doubt that several of the leaders of the Church in the early part of this dispensation believed and taught that Jesus was married. We do not need to explain or defend them.

However, we also recognize that many leaders of the Church have also cautioned us about speculating on issues that the scrip-tures have not addressed.

In the end, it would not bother modern disciples who are firmly rooted in the doctrines and ordinances of the kingdom to find out one day that Jesus was married while on earth. Eternal marriage is one of the most ennobling doctrines in our Heavenly Father's plan of happiness (see Doctrine and Covenants 132).

Someday we will know all things and have our questions answered. The Lord has promised that there is "a time to come in the which nothing shall be withheld, whether there be one God or many gods, they shall be manifest. All thrones and dominions, principalities and powers, shall be revealed and set forth upon *all who have endured valiantly for the gospel of Jesus Christ*" (Doctrine and Covenants 121:28–29; emphasis added). But therein is found the ultimate point. If we have not studied and applied in our lives the profundity of the Atonement of our Lord and come to know for a certainty of His divinity, no other information we acquire about Him will make any difference.

CHAPTER 4

The Search for the Holy Grail

"The legend of the Holy Grail is a legend about royal blood.
When Grail legend speaks of 'the chalice that held the blood of
Christ' . . . it speaks, in fact, of Mary Magdalene—the female
womb that carried Jesus' royal bloodline."

(*The Da Vinci Code,* p. 249).

Boiled down to the simplest terms, *The Da Vinci Code* is
another fictional account of a recurring theme in Western
civilization—the quest for the Holy Grail. However, here the Grail
story goes in a different direction from previous tales. *The Da
Vinci Code*'s Holy Grail is a function of the marriage of Jesus and
Mary Magdalene; it is a product of their union. But, more importantly, it is also the object of a long and profound conspiracy.

An undergirding theme of the novel is that the true identification of the Grail has been kept hidden for centuries, through a
cover-up involving the Vatican. Others in ages past have not
found the real Holy Grail because they did not understand what it
really was. In previous versions of the legend, the Grail was variously identified as a cup or chalice used at the Last Supper, a vessel containing the blood Christ shed on the Cross, a silver dish, a
stone from heaven, a sword, spear, or lance, a secret book, or many
other things. But *The Da Vinci Code* declares that the identity of
the real Grail has been the object of "the greatest cover-up in
human history. Not only was Jesus Christ married," says the character named Teabing, "but He was a father [and] Mary Magdalene

was the Holy Vessel. . . . She was the womb that bore the lineage" (*The Da Vinci Code,* p. 249). Thus, in *The Da Vinci Code,* the entire story of the search for the Holy Grail is the search for royal blood descended from Jesus.

The Grail in History

The quest to understand and find the Holy Grail has been a moving force in history for over a thousand years. The Holy Grail has been presented in many forms from medieval times onward. The exact origins of the Grail legend are shrouded in mystery. In what are believed to be the earliest medieval forms of the story, the Grail was some type of magical dish or cup that produced special food and that was an object of healing or regeneration. Such ideas are traced back to classical and early Celtic myths that contain images of horns of plenty and magic cauldrons that restore life. The word *Grail* appears to derive from the Old French word *graal,* which was a form of the Latin *gradalis,* denoting a wide-mouthed or shallow vessel.

The first extant written text about the Grail was composed in the late twelfth century by a French poet named Chrétien de Troyes. Entitled *Conte del Graal,* it is the story of a young, innocent knight, Perceval (Parzival), who happens upon a castle in a remote valley. His host, an invalid bound to his couch, invites him to stay the evening, and as they are having dinner, a strange procession passes through the room. First comes a man carrying a white lance, from which a drop of blood falls onto Perceval's hand. The lance carrier is followed by two more squires, each bearing golden candelabra. Next, a beautiful young woman passes by, holding in her hands a *graal,* a gold vessel beset with precious gems. She is followed by another maiden carrying a silver platter.

Perceval is curious but says nothing because of his overzealous but misguided desire to follow the chivalric virtue of silence. The next day he leaves the castle, comes across a young woman

Perceval (Parzival) and the Search for the Holy Grail, 1912, Ferdinand Leeke, private possession. The saintly knight, Parzival, serves as a central figure in many of the medieval Grail romances and is a companion of Sirs Gawain, Galahad, and Lancelot, each of whom sought for spiritual enlightenment. *Used by Permission, Erich Lessing/Art Resource, NY*

mourning the loss of her lover, and is told he (Perceval) has been at the castle of the Fisher King, his host who had been crippled in battle. Had the knight been perceptive enough to ask the meaning of the *graal,* he is informed, he would have met the test set before him and been the instrument of restoring the Fisher King as well as the surrounding wasteland to health. The knight continues his wanderings, and after five unfruitful years comes to a hermitage, begs help from a holy man there, and learns that the Fisher King is Perceval's uncle, whose father's life was renewed by the contents of the *graal* or Grail that Perceval had seen earlier.

Chrétien died without finishing his Grail story, but it was picked up by others who wrote a number of tales and attached greater Christian significance to the developing legend. In one of the most famous versions of the story, written about A.D. 1200 by a Burgundian poet named Robert de Boron and entitled *Joseph d'Arimathie,* the story of the Grail begins with Joseph of Arimathea. According to the story, Joseph came to possess the very cup used by Jesus to administer the sacrament or Eucharist at the Last Supper. Joseph then used the cup to catch the blood of Christ as He hung on the cross while the disciples looked on the grisly scene, powerless. Joseph of Arimathea, it will be remembered, was a wealthy member of the Sanhedrin who helped prepare Jesus' body for burial and provided the tomb that became His resting place (Matthew 27:57–60).

As the fictional story progresses, Joseph of Arimathea is imprisoned by the Romans because he is a follower of Jesus Christ. While in prison, Joseph is able to survive, thanks to the magical Grail. After being freed, Joseph leads a group of Christians who carried the Grail to the Holy Land. He finally brings the Grail to Britain, where it is guarded by Joseph's descendants, a succession of Grail Kings, in the castle Joseph builds called Corbenic Castle.

Robert de Boron's tale, written in verse, is based on late apocryphal texts, the *Evangelium Nicodemi* (*Gospel of Nicodemus*) and

THE SEARCH FOR THE HOLY GRAIL

the *Vindicta Salvatoris* (*Vengeance of the Lord*). It was in the thirteenth century that the word *holy* began to be used more consistently to describe the Grail, precisely because the Grail became identified with the story of Joseph of Arimathea. Moreover, scholars also recognize that de Boron connects the conversion, or evangelization at least, of Britain to the presence of the Grail in that land.

In prose versions of Robert de Boron's works, as well as in later Grail romances, the Grail story is linked more closely to Arthurian legend. In the foremost French Grail story, a work entitled *La Queste del Saint Graal* (*Quest for the Holy Grail*), Chrétien's Perceval is joined by a new hero—the morally pure Sir Galahad. Other knights with familiar names are found in various versions of the story: Gawain, Bors, and Lancelot. The quest for the Holy Grail becomes a main adventure of King Arthur's Knights of the Round Table—a search for a mystical union with God. The essence of *La Queste del Saint Graal* was used by Sir Thomas Malory in the fifteenth century to create his prose classic *Le Morte d'Arthur.*

As these later versions of the Grail quest unfold, the Knights of the Round Table decide to search Britain for the Holy Grail after seeing a vision of it suspended in the air. They pass through dangerous adventures in their quest. After searching for years, three knights, the purest and most morally perfect among men (Galahad is one of them), along with nine men from other countries, enter Corbenic Castle. There they see a vision of Joseph of Arimathea appearing as a priest. Angels bring in the Grail as well as the bloody spear that had pierced Christ's side during the Crucifixion. Then Christ emerges from the cup and gives communion to the men. After leaving the castle, the three knights sail away on the ship that, they discover, carries the Grail. The ship takes the knights to a distant city where Galahad dies, and the other two see the Grail rise into heaven.

It is not difficult to see how the legends of the Holy Grail developed and evolved in medieval Christendom. The dish or vessel once believed to be imbued with magical and regenerative properties ultimately became an unquestionable Christian relic, pointing more intensely to Jesus Christ, the Savior and Giver of eternal life. There is an impressive progression from the *graal* of Chrétien's story to the cup used by Jesus at the Last Supper and the chalice that held Christ's holy blood, to an object that bestowed God's grace as well as profound visions, and then to the vessel out of which came the actual person of Christ.

One interesting and different development in the history of the evolution of the legend of the Holy Grail comes in the epic tale *Parzival,* written by German poet Wolfram von Eschenbach (ca. 1210). In his version, the Grail is a stone guarded by the Knights Templar. The stone has magical powers bringing health and eternal youth. Though sounding pagan in nature, the power of the stone comes from a small white wafer brought by a dove every year on Good Friday.

It was perfectly natural for von Eschenbach to make the Templars the guardians of the Grail stone. *The Da Vinci Code* also recognizes them. They were an actual order of knightly monks, devoted to the protection of Christian pilgrims and travelers in the Holy Land. King Baldwin II of Jerusalem, one of the rulers of the Crusader kingdoms, or Latin Kingdoms, in the Holy Land, installed the Templars in a wing of the king's palace, a former mosque in the Jerusalem Temple precinct. This gave them their name, the Order of the Poor Knights of the Temple of Solomon of Jerusalem (established ca. A.D. 1119). As knights who fought for God, they became legendary, though their position financially and strategically was precarious at first. However, in 1128 a preceptory (a cross between a monastery and a recruiting office) was built for the Templars in London and rebuilt in 1185 after the first one burned down. It is this Templar Church that is one of the backdrops in *The Da Vinci Code*'s plot.

The kingdom of Jerusalem was lost to Muslim warriors in 1187, causing the Templars to relocate to the city of Acre (across the bay from modern Haifa) and compelling Richard the Lionheart to mount a crusade to regain Jerusalem. Eventually, the Templars were driven from Palestine altogether and went to Cyprus. The Templars became wealthy by fostering a financial relationship with the French crown. The latter developed a dependence on Templar loans and is probably why *The Da Vinci Code* mentions, mistakenly, that the Templars were the first bankers in Europe. Actually, Jewish merchants are probably due this honor. Still, the Templar bank in Paris was one of the busiest in Europe.

With the major crusades over by the fourteenth century, the Templars' reason for existence was finished. They refused to merge with the Knights Hospitallers, and, in 1307, King Philip IV of France had all Templars within France arrested. They were mostly old, unarmed men, but they controlled land and financial resources needed by the crown. The arrest of all Templars outside of France occurred shortly thereafter. The order may have been ending, but the legends about the Templars were, in effect, reaching their apex. They were larger-than-life warriors for Christ. They established almost impossible standards to live by—bravery, purity, and piety. But the wonder of it all is that some of them managed to live up to these standards. Not surprisingly, von Eschenbach made them the guardians of the Grail castle in his epic poem, *Parzival.* Von Eschenbach had visited the Holy Land in 1218, and the knights captured his imagination.

In fact, the image of these faithful and true knights, wearing white cloaks with red crosses on their shoulder, has lasted into modern times. In the twentieth century, modern books and films such as *Indiana Jones and the Last Crusade* (1989) have reinforced the image of the Templars as the protectors of the Holy Grail. *The Da Vinci Code* employs this general image.

With the coming of the Reformation, the Holy Grail disappeared from the poetic imagination for a time. However, two centuries later, it appeared in a new form—secret societies. Groups such as the Rosicrucians and the Freemasons borrowed from the romantic and mystical tales of previous ages and employed the powerful symbols of these works. The Grail legends continued to exert a powerful influence on works of literature and art created by authors and artists of the nineteenth and twentieth centuries, including Alfred Lord Tennyson and Mark Twain. In Germany, Wagner's opera *Parsifal* revived interest in national origins combined with Christian symbols and images. Because of Stephen Spielberg's *Indiana Jones* epic, an entirely new generation has linked the Grail quest with its Templar guardians.

The Da Vinci Code Grail

The medieval Grail legends constitute a marvelous chapter in the history of moral fiction. The Grail stories build on one another, adding successive layers, but always seeming to point more forcefully back to Jesus Christ as the anchor of their audience's faith and hope and author of their salvation. The Grail legends progressively remind their audiences of the virtues, values, principles, and concepts that were the ideal in medieval Christianity and that epitomized the pure, perfectly moral life of the true Christian warrior.

In legend, only those whose motives and actions were pure were successful in their quest for the Holy Grail. Those, like Gawain, who did not seek God's grace or help failed in their quest. So, too, with Lancelot, who, because of his adultery with Queen Guinevere, could see the Holy Grail only in a dream. Knights Perceval, Bors, and Galahad received the highest, most impressive, revelations.

In many ways, *The Da Vinci Code* is another step in the history of the development of the Grail legends. It presents some of the elements found in earlier incarnations of the story. But there are significant differences. Obviously, we immediately recognize the major difference in the identification of the Grail—what the term refers to. But in *The Da Vinci Code*, it isn't just a difference in identity; it is a complete reorientation of the quest.

Sir Galahad and the other Grail knights were searching for the chalice of the Last Supper, the cup that held the blood of Christ, because they sought communion with God and desired to kneel before Him with pure hearts. In *The Da Vinci Code*, "the quest for the Holy Grail is literally the quest to kneel before the bones of Mary Magdalene" (*The Da Vinci Code*, p. 257). Therein lies the tale of two opposite quests.

The quest for the Grail in *The Da Vinci Code* is not a search for salvation or even spiritual enlightenment, through contact with relics connected to Jesus Christ, but is a search to find the "lost sacred feminine." However, in reorienting us, the novel manipulates and misrepresents the very intent of the earlier Grail stories. The character Langdon explains: "The Grail is literally the ancient symbol for womanhood, and the *Holy* Grail represents the sacred feminine and . . . is symbolic of the lost goddess. When Christianity came along, the old pagan religions did not die easily. Legends of chivalric quests for the lost Grail were in fact stories of forbidden quests to find the lost sacred feminine. Knights who claimed to be 'searching for the chalice' were speaking in code as a way to protect themselves from a Church that had subjugated women, banished the Goddess, burned nonbelievers, and forbidden the pagan reverence for the sacred feminine" (*The Da Vinci Code*, pp. 238–39).

All of this certainly would have come as news to the authors of the Grail romances. It is fortunate they did not have *The Da Vinci Code* there telling them what their quest really was and thereby depriving the world of one of the great cycles of ennobling literature.

CHAPTER 5

The Story of Mary Magdalene

"The Church needed to defame Mary
Magdalene in order to cover up her dangerous secret—
her role as the Holy Grail."

(*The Da Vinci Code*, p. 244)

Apart from Jesus' mother, Mary, Mary Magdalene is one of the most recognizable women disciples in the New Testament. Her faith and dedication to the Lord have continued to attract the attention of subsequent generations. This chapter will outline what is known about the historical person Mary Magdalene, separating the historical person from the later legendary accounts about her.

Mary's name in the Gospel accounts is almost universally given as Mariam the Magdalene (the only two exceptions are found in John 20:1, 18), which is translated popularly as Mary Magdalene. Many scholars feel that her name suggests a connection to the city of Magdala, an important commercial city on the western shore of the Sea of Galilee (possibly the town of "Tarichaeae" as mentioned by Josephus) north of Tiberius and south of Capernaum. In the Jewish world, where individuals did not have both first and second names, various conventions were invented to help distinguish individuals by identifying their relationships to others, as is the case with "Simon Bar-jona" (meaning Simon son of Jonah; Matthew 16:17), or their place of origin—for example, "Jesus of Nazareth." In this reconstruction, we should assume that what is intended by the twofold name is that she is "Mary of Magdala."

Luke, who had seen that Mary Magdalene appears abruptly at the end of the Gospel of Mark, introduced her into his telling of the story earlier than Mark had done (see Mark 15:40). Luke does not provide his readers any details about the initial meeting between Jesus and Mary. However, no other Gospel author introduces Mary Magdalene as early into his Gospel account as Luke does.

Although we cannot know for certain why Luke may have done so, he likely wanted to clarify what seemed to be ambiguous in the other Gospel accounts that mention other Marys. Mary Magdalene went to the tomb of Jesus, but for what reasons did she go there? Luke may have sought to answer the question of when Mary Magdalene became a disciple of Jesus and what role she played in His ministry.

Luke probably never considered that a future generation would ask whether Jesus was married to Mary Magdalene or whether the two had any personal relationship beyond Master and disciple. To Luke, clarifying her exact relationship to Jesus meant explaining that she financially supported Jesus' ministry and that she, along with "Joanna the wife of Chuza Herod's steward, and Susanna, and many others, . . . ministered unto him of their substance" (Luke 8:2–3). Unlike many of Jesus' other disciples, Mary Magdalene played an important part in financing Jesus' three-year public ministry during which Jesus was completely dedicated to the work of teaching, preaching, and healing. Her financial support reveals not only her personal convictions about Jesus' teachings but also something of her financial well-being. All other references to Mary Magdalene in the Gospels associate her with the events at the cross and the tomb, clearly showing that she was one

The Crucifixion

Mary Magdalene at the Crucifixion, early seventeenth century A.D., Anthony van Dyck, Musée du Louvre, Paris. The earliest sources for the life and ministry of Jesus of Nazareth are the New Testament texts. In the Gospels, women play an important role in the narrative. Of the women, Mary Magdalene is highlighted as a committed disciple of Jesus; she was at the cross and the empty tomb. *Used by permission, Erich Lessing/Art Resource, NY* of the inner circle of Jesus' followers during the last months of His ministry.

It is highly unlikely that Luke could ever have imagined the kinds of legends and stories that would become part of the apocryphal traditions of the early Christian Church—traditions that eventually gave way to further embellishments that solidified during medieval Christianity and that eventually were reinterpreted as part of a modern proclivity to highlight the sensational and question the Gospels themselves.

The Gospels seem to be careful whenever they speak of Mary Magdalene to include both identifying indicators because of the possible confusion among the many Marys mentioned in the New Testament.

In the Gospels, Jesus' mother, Lazarus's sister, and the wife of Cleophas were all named Mary; therefore, the authors had to develop some means of differentiating Mary Magdalene from the others. This need for distinction is not surprising when we realize that tomb inscriptions from Judea and Galilee attest to the popularity of the name *Mary* in the first century. Some scholars report that nearly 40 percent of women were given the name of Mary or Elizabeth at birth.

The name *Mary Magdalene* possibly was not used during her lifetime but is only a convention of the written Gospels to help readers and listeners distinguish among the Marys of the New Testament Gospels.

Discussions of Mary Magdalene's relationship to Jesus are found in the four Gospel accounts. According to the Gospel of Mark, Jesus died at about the ninth hour, or roughly three o'clock, and He then hung on the cross for some time afterwards. Following Jewish custom at the time, Jesus' body would have had to be taken down from the cross, washed, wrapped, and embalmed before sundown. To emphasize that the followers of Jesus faced a serious obstacle with the approach of the Sabbath, Mark also records that Joseph of

Arimathea sought out Pilate and requested that Joseph be permitted to care for Jesus' body. Assuming that he had to make the
request, return to the site of the Crucifixion, care for the body, and
transport it to the place of burial in two or three hours, we realize
that the disciples were likely rushed in their preparations.

Mark's careful attention to the time when the events of the
Crucifixion and Resurrection took place continues in the accounts
where the women disciples visit the tomb. Mark reports the time
of that visit as "when the sabbath was past . . . and very early in
the morning the first day of the week" (Mark 16:1–2). Mark provided these details for a specific reason. From his report, we can
be certain that the women who visited the tomb in no way vio-
lated the Jewish Sabbath, which ended at sunrise on Sunday
morning. In his preparations of Jesus' body, Joseph of Arimathea
was rushed, and now, following the Jewish Sabbath, some of Jesus'
closest disciples had returned to finish those preparations. Two of
the Gospels' authors clearly make this the purpose of the women's
return visit to the tomb on Sunday morning, explaining that the
women carried spices with them to finish embalming Jesus' body
(Mark 16:1; Luke 24:1). Mary Magdalene, along with a handful
of other faithful disciples, returned to complete what they had
done for Jesus during the earthly ministry. They intended to take
care of His physical needs.

What is remarkable in all these stories is that Mary Magdalene
is always mentioned as being among the first persons at the tomb;
in one case, she is identified as the first person at the tomb (see
John 20:1). Even when mentioned as part of a group who arrived
at the tomb that morning, Mary Magdalene is always specifically
mentioned by name while the others are not. She was almost certainly the leader of the group. Given her prominent role, perhaps
she is the one who came up with the idea that they complete the
task of caring for Jesus' body. For reasons now forgotten and lost,
the authors of the Gospels remembered that her presence at the

tomb was unique and that she stood apart from the other women disciples. That is not to imply that any of the Gospel authors hinted that Mary had anything other than a Master-disciple relationship with Jesus, but they unanimously affirm that her discipleship was truly remarkable.

The author of the Gospel of John, who was perhaps Jesus' closest personal acquaintance, also remembered Mary Magdalene in a way the other Gospel writers did not. In John's account, Mary not only is among the first persons at the tomb but also is the first person to see and touch the resurrected Savior. When all the others had departed after seeing the empty tomb, Mary Magdalene remained. She may have lingered because her heart had been broken by a devastating loss and now an apparent theft of her Lord's remains. Her lingering was rewarded with an appearance of the resurrected Jesus.

To John, it was simply not enough to relate that she had seen the Lord, but he also records a very touching conversation between the two. To emphasize Mary's emotional strain, John recorded that she was weeping as she bent down to look in the empty tomb a second time (see John 20:11). As she turned away from the tomb, she saw the resurrected Savior, whom she mistook to be the gardener. To the supposed gardener, she said, "Sir, if thou have borne him hence, tell me where thou hast laid him, and I will take him away" (John 20:15). Her request was both formal and direct. She had already heard Jesus' voice, which she did not recognize, but the moment He said her name she knew it was the Lord (see John 20:16). Something in Jesus' intonation, not necessarily His appearance, made her recognize Him.

After her initial wave of recognition, Mary called him "Rabboni," a rather formal term that would be translated as "Master" (John 20:16). Unfortunately, the King James Version then confuses what transpired next. Jesus immediately said to her, "Do not hold on to me" or "You cannot keep me back by holding me," implying that Mary had embraced the Savior. He gently reminded her that He was no longer of this world (see John 20:17). Mary Magdalene then obediently returned and reported her experience to the disciples. Fortunately, the Apostle John, himself one of Jesus' closest disciples, did not exclude this moment of profound discipleship, even though it did not involve him. The only other event to rival the intimacy of this one was when Jesus spoke to another Mary, His mother, from the cross.

The Gospel authors preserve only one other detail from the life of Mary Magdalene. Luke 8:2 and Mark 16:9 both confirm that Mary had "seven devils" cast out of her and that some of the other women disciples who aided Jesus had also been healed of infirmities. An account of her healing is not given in the Gospels, but the event probably took place during Jesus' Galilean ministry. Perhaps Luke intentionally linked the reference to her healing with the statement of how she aided Jesus financially as a way of explaining her motivations for doing so. She had been deeply converted through a miraculous healing, and she faithfully followed the Lord thereafter.

We find no other references to Mary Magdalene in the New Testament. Two Gospel authors record stories about sinful women who met Jesus, but we find no hint that these women had any relationship to Mary Magdalene. Luke records the story of the woman who washed Jesus' feet with her tears and dried them with her hair (see Luke 7:36–50), and John relates the story of the woman who was caught in adultery and was subsequently brought to Jesus for judgment (see John 8:1–11). Although these two women were in no way associated with Mary Magdalene in the New Testament, they do become important in later discussions about her life, particularly during the medieval period.

Apocryphal Accounts of Mary Magdalene

That Mary Magdalene became an important figure in early Christianity after the close of the New Testament period is confirmed

through the existence of a gospel forged in her name. Several apocryphal gospels also build on the traditions about Mary found in the
canonical Gospels. Generally, these apocryphal accounts report traditions about Mary regarding two separate themes: her special relationship with Jesus and her witness of the Resurrection. Post-New
Testament speculation on these two subjects shows that Christians,
in general, were intrigued by the possibility that Mary may have
been taught secret truths during her time alone with Jesus in the
garden after He appeared to her at the empty tomb. Often, later
texts build up the idea that Jesus and Mary had a unique relationship—on the basis of her being one of two named women who
supported Jesus financially and also because she was the leader of
those who visited the empty tomb to take care of His mortal body.

In the Gnostic *Gospel of Mary*, which was discovered among
the Nag Hammadi codices, Mary appears as a revelatory figure.
The document itself was likely composed in the late second century or early third century A.D., perhaps in Egypt. Scholars are
divided on exactly how early this text should be dated, but we
have no evidence suggesting that it is earlier than our canonical
sources. In fact, the gospel builds upon the stereotypes of Peter
and Mary Magdalene established in the canonical Gospel tradition. Unfortunately, only a few leaves of the original remain,
therefore making it difficult to make any firm conclusions about
dating and provenance.

In this gospel, Mary Magdalene is in the presence of several
of the Apostles—Peter, Andrew, and Levi—where she gives them
instructions on some of Jesus' teachings. Her ability to interpret
the teachings of Jesus is the result of a vision wherein she was
shown the ascent of the soul into heaven. She taught the disciples
that sin should not be understood as a moral issue; instead, sin
leads to the enslavement of the soul in the hereafter and inhibits it
during its ascent through the heavenly realms. Peter, who is star-
tled that Mary would have such superior knowledge, questions

whether such information is really from God. Somewhat incredu-
lously, Peter asks, "Did he really speak with a woman without our
knowledge (and) not openly? Are we to turn about and all listen to
her? Did he prefer her to us?"[1]

Following the pattern of other Gnostic discourses, Mary sees
the Savior and is taught special things. Her vision, like so many
others in the apocryphal literature, reveals how the soul will
ascend through the heavenly spheres. Any soul that is corrupt will
be kept back, and only the purest of souls will be able to return
unhindered. Often, Gnostic revelatory discourses teach the listener
how to pass by heavenly powers or angels. These angelic interme-
diaries impede the progress of souls who have become too reliant
on the physical world.

Peter, who is included as a metaphor of the established
Church hierarchy, and Andrew, who likewise represents apostolic
Christianity, openly oppose Mary. Levi or Matthew is the person-
ification of the written Gospels, and it is he who defends Mary's
revelation. In other words, apostolic traditions and teachings reject
what Mary reveals, but the Gospels support her. The *Gospel of
Mary* presents an alternative to previously established Christian
practice. In this context, we can properly understand Peter's rejec-
tion of her witness. He, representing the apostolic tradition,
rebukes her, whereas Levi/Matthew, representing the textual
tradition, supports her. Levi/Matthew concludes the discussion,
saying, "Surely the Savior knows her very well. That is why he
loved her more than us."[2] Although the information in the *Gospel
of Mary* is late and secondary, it does build upon the earlier canonical Gospel accounts, which imply that Mary had a special knowledge of Jesus that was given to her in the garden of the empty
tomb.

Another secondary apocryphal gospel, the *Gospel of Philip*,
reports information that is remarkably similar to that of the *Gospel
of Mary*. The *Gospel of Philip* clearly derives from the New

Testament Gospels and quotes from them directly in several instances. That it may contain early traditions is possible, but those traditions have been recast in a Gnostic framework. More than likely, this gospel is later than the *Gospel of Mary* and should be dated to the mid-second century or later. Mary Magdalene appears only in passing in the *Gospel of Philip*.

Perhaps the most scintillating information in the *Gospel of Philip* comes from the passage that reports, "And the companion of the [. . .] Mary Magdalene. [. . . loved] her more than [all] the disciples [and used to] kiss her [often] on her [. . .]".[3] As previously indicated, the brackets represent holes in the text, and words that appear in brackets here are not present in the manuscript but were placed there in an attempt to restore the text to the extent possible. In fact, the phrase *and used to* and the word *often* are conjectural emendations of the text.

The restored text gives the impression that Jesus kissed her on a regular basis, suggesting that their relationship was uniquely intimate. However, if we remove the conjectural emendations and read only the visible text, the passage should read, "he kissed her on her . . ." Of course, without the final word, we cannot know what the author intended. But he may simply have said that Jesus kissed her on the forehead or, more imaginatively, on the hand, but "often on the mouth" is simply stretching the evidence too far.

So far, we can verify that one of the common themes in the Gnostic traditions about Mary Magdalene, and indeed in other Gnostic texts about women in general, is that an underlying correction of the perceived male-dominated ecclesiastical tradition is evident. We consistently see the theme in the literature about Mary, that Jesus loved her more than He loved any of the other disciples, even more than He loved Peter or John. Moreover, Mary's status as the beloved disciple is not derived from a special physical relationship with Jesus, such as marriage, but instead is the result of a revelation or vision from which she is able to rival the male disciples. This corrective tradition can be seen in one of the earliest apocryphal texts, the *Gospel of Thomas.*

Here, Peter again complains about Mary Magdalene's prominent position among the disciples and hopes that Jesus will exclude her from their discussions. However, instead of a positive endorsement of women disciples, the *Gospel of Thomas* teaches that Mary will have to be transformed into a male before she can achieve a status equal to Peter's. This interaction is recorded in the final saying of this gospel: "Simon Peter said to them, 'Let Mary leave us, for females are not worthy of life.' Jesus said, 'Behold, I shall guide her to make her male, so that she too may become a living spirit resembling you males. For every female who makes herself male will enter the kingdom of heaven.'"[4]

Probably earlier than the *Gospel of Mary* or the *Gospel of Philip,* the apocryphal *Gospel of Thomas* contains a very pointed denunciation of female disciples in general. Perhaps in the first century after the death of Jesus, such a radical denunciation of women was accepted in more esoteric fringe traditions where sayings like these would be interpreted in a manner that downplayed its obvious misogynistic stance. But to the larger community of Christian believers, this type of rhetoric would have been highly unpopular. Later Gnostic texts attempt to counter Mary Magdalene's negative image by making her a revealer of secret wisdom and a corrector of ecclesiastical traditions.

Potentially, some of the earliest recollections about Mary Magdalene after the New Testament texts come from two apocryphal writings, the *Epistula Apostolorum* and the *Gospel of Peter.* The first, a clearly anti-Gnostic text from the second century, records this tradition about the women who went to the tomb of Jesus: "He was buried in a place which is called the place of the skull to which three women came, Sarah, Martha and Mary Magdalene. They carried ointment to pour out upon his body, weeping and mourning over what had happened. And they approached the tomb and found the stone where it had been rolled away from the tomb, and they opened the door and did not find his body. And as they were mourning and weeping, the Lord appeared to them and said to them, do not weep; I am he whom you seek. But let one of you go to your brothers and say to them, 'Come, our Master has risen from the dead.' And Mary came to us and told us. And we said to her, 'What have we to do with you, O woman? He that is dead and buried, can he then live? And we did not believe her.'"[5] Each of the three women disciples mentioned in this account returns to the Apostles and reports what each had seen and heard at the tomb. The Apostles, who are reluctant to believe any of their reports, are eventually convinced when they are permitted to see the same things.

The tradition about Mary is not static, which is a direct result of there being two ancient versions of the text, one preserved in Ethiopic and one in Coptic. In neither of these versions was Mary Magdalene the first at the tomb, nor is she the leader of the group as she is in the canonical Gospel accounts. But she does travel with the Lord to meet the Apostles and convinces them that she was telling the truth. This account likely preserves an early oral tradition that included the names of some of the other women who visited the tomb—Sarah and Mary. Later Catholic traditions confused Mary Magdalene with Mary of Bethany, and perhaps this early tradition provides the origin of the confusion. Mary of Bethany had a sister named Martha. In this account, Mary Magdalene comes to the tomb with Martha, which could easily be confused as a reference to the two sisters Mary and Martha of Bethany rather than Mary Magdalene and Martha of Bethany.

One of the earliest commentaries on Mary Magdalene's visit to the tomb as it is recorded in the canonical Gospels is found in the *Gospel of Peter*. Just as in the canonical reports, Mary Magdalene came to the tomb very early on Sunday morning to take care of the body of Jesus. However, unlike the canonical accounts that only hint at her reasons for going to the tomb, the *Gospel of Peter* explicitly states her reasons for doing so. It records: "Mary Magdalene, a woman disciple of the Lord—for fear of the Jews, since (they) were inflamed with wrath, she had not done at the sepulchre of the Lord what woman are wont to do for those beloved of them who die—took with her her women friends and came to the sepulchre where he was laid."[6]

Two specific details emerge from this account that are not readily apparent elsewhere: the other women who visited the tomb were Mary's friends, and the embalming of Jesus' body was delayed because they feared that the Jews would retaliate against them for their actions. Whether these details are as early as the canonical accounts is a matter of debate, but they almost certainly rely on early oral traditions about Mary Magdalene. They are credible details, and they do not contain the overtly Gnostic flavor of some of the other apocryphal accounts.

To summarize the portrait of Mary Magdalene in the apocrypha, we would be wise to say that potentially three details emerge that have some historical value. First, Mary and the other women disciples may have felt threatened when they visited the tomb on Sunday morning. Their actions on the Friday of Jesus' death may also have been curtailed out of fear of retaliation against Jesus' disciples. Second, oral tradition may have supplied two of the names of the women who visited the tomb with Mary Magdalene—Sarah and Martha. Third, the women who visited the tomb with Mary Magdalene may have been her personal friends.

Later apocryphal traditions record the belief that Mary was given a special revelation that she later communicated to the Twelve Apostles. These disciples, who were hesitant to accept her testimony, eventually came to the conclusion that Jesus loved her more than He loved them; therefore, her testimony was likely credible. This pattern is prominent in later texts and might be part of a larger cycle of events associated with Mary Magdalene. No other details surface about Mary Magdalene or her personal relationship with Jesus. By the fourth century A.D., Mary Magdalene had become a powerful literary figure in Gnostic Christian circles. Whether that popularity had been transferred into orthodox Christian circles is unclear. However, the later reaction by Catholic Christianity makes it seem obvious that they were attempting to suppress her inflated image.

The Suppression of Mary Magdalene in Later Traditions

One of the surprising details in the history of the traditions associated with Mary Magdalene is that during the first few centuries, reports about her tended to elevate her importance and status, whereas later reports universally suppress the earlier positive portrayals. The historical reasons for these actions are not entirely clear, but we see the plausibility that Catholic Christianity reacted to the overly positive traditions about her preserved in Gnostic literature.

Beginning as early as the third century, in the writings of Tertullian and later Jerome and Augustine, Mary Magdalene began to be associated with the sinful woman of Luke 7. In Luke's account, a woman "which was a sinner" entered into the home where Jesus was eating, bringing with her an alabaster jar containing ointment, and began "to wash his feet with tears, and did wipe them with the hairs of her head, and kissed his feet, and anointed them with the ointment" (Luke 7:37–38). Rebuking Jesus, the Pharisees questioned whether Jesus could really be a prophet because He should have known what type of woman she was—a sinner—and therefore He should not have permitted her to have such intimate contact with Him. At the end of the account, Jesus taught those present that her sins had been forgiven and that her faith had saved her (see Luke 7:47–50).

Two elements emerge about the identity of this unnamed

woman follower: she had formerly been a sinner, and she obviously had great love for Jesus. These two elements were apparently significant enough for some commentators in the third and fourth centuries to suggest that she was really Mary Magdalene, who also loved the Savior and who had been healed of "seven devils" (Luke 8:2). Although we can see no direct historical link between the two women, the fact that both had been healed in one way—one from her sins and the other from spiritual possession—was sufficient to suggest they were the same person. Luke was probably unaware of any such historical relationship in his account because he does not introduce Mary Magdalene until the next chapter when it would have been more logical to make the connection when he first introduced her into the story. We end up with no reason to believe they were the same woman.

In A.D. 591, Pope Gregory I "the Great" made a pontifical declaration that Mary Magdalene was the same person as Mary of Bethany who was the same as the repentant sinner in Luke 7, thereby collapsing three separate individuals into a single person. Popular speculation about the sin of the woman in Luke 7 also suggested that she had been a prostitute prior to washing the Savior's feet with her tears. This popular notion was then transferred to Mary Magdalene through her connection with the repentant sinner. By the sixth century, it was common to think of Mary Magdalene as a repentant prostitute.

A further confusion of Mary Magdalene's identity took place in the Middle Ages when some commentators made a further connection between her and the woman caught in adultery in John 8. In that event, a small group of Pharisees brought to Jesus a woman whom they had caught in the very act of adultery. They had hoped that Jesus would make some declaration of how she should be judged according to the law. In one of the best-known scenes from the New Testament, Jesus asked those present to consider their own sins before carrying out their proposed sentence on her.

Although the author of the Gospel of John knew Mary Magdalene by name and mentions her on several occasions, he gave no hint that this otherwise unidentified woman was Mary Magdalene. In fact, at the end of the account, the woman departs and never appears again in the Gospel. From a reader's perspective, she literally disappears from the story, and we are left to wonder what became of her. If John knew of any later stories of this woman's actions, he neglected to report them. He was obviously aware of Mary Magdalene, but his knowledge of the woman caught in adultery appears to be limited to this single event.

At the end of the sixth century, this composite portrait of Mary Magdalene had reached a climax. She was, in the minds of thousands of Christians, a repentant former prostitute who had been healed through a remarkable act of faith. She was also blessed with a personal visitation of the Savior at the tomb. This new merged identity helped Mary Magdalene become the ideal repentant sinner in medieval Christianity, a person with whom everyday individuals could relate.

While the literary portrait of Mary developed, so did her iconography. In the Middle Ages, depictions of Mary Magdalene abounded, and she is variously depicted as the patron saint of sinners. She is typically shown with long brown hair and is always beautiful. Only Jesus' mother is depicted as being as beautiful as Mary Magdalene. During the Baroque, Renaissance, and other periods, her portraiture followed the development of the day, but her age in those depictions is fixed. Although Jesus could be portrayed as very young or middle-aged and although Joseph was often depicted as elderly, Mary Magdalene's portraiture is static. Mary is also almost always shown as being alone.

July 22 has been established in Catholic tradition as a day to commemorate the repentant sinner Mary Magdalene, and priests and bishops recite a collection of readings from Luke 7 and John 20 during the liturgy. In the mass held every July, therefore, listeners have been continually reminded of the direct association between the unnamed repentant sinner and Mary Magdalene who came to the tomb of Jesus. As a result of careful Catholic New Testament scholarship that had untangled the web of misunderstandings about her, the collection of readings was changed in 1969, thus officially putting an end to any direct connection between Mary Magdalene and the unnamed woman in Luke 7.

But by then, the Church's literary portrait of Mary Magdalene had helped endear her to the masses, which resulted in a proliferation of icons and portraits of her. Interestingly, depictions of her abound in the Middle Ages, but she is entirely absent in the earliest Christian paintings. Although depictions of her in the first few centuries of Christian art were likely made by artists, not a single example has survived. Not until after the confusion of the Marys occurs in the sixth century and later did portraits of her begin to appear quite regularly. From the surviving artwork in the first three centuries A.D., we can see that Christians focused on a few specific themes: the Resurrected Savior, the Last Supper, Jesus as the good shepherd, and the parables of Jesus. Other images do appear from this era, but they appear randomly. Perhaps new discoveries will reveal that Christians depicted Mary and other women followers of Jesus in the earliest decades after His resurrection. However, from the existing evidence, we know early art was focused on Jesus and His life. Christians were particularly interested in the events from the last week of His life. Only later did Christian artists expand their interest to include individuals from less-prominent stories.

Unfortunately, we no longer have enough information to establish definitively the reasons why Mary's positive portrait in the New Testament was subsequently repainted in medieval Christianity. Those responsible may have been reacting to the legendary figure of Mary that had become popular in Gnostic Christianity, or they may have simply been attempting to fill out the incomplete New Testament accounts. During the period in which Mary began to be confused with the other Marys in the New Testament and with the unnamed women in Luke and John, it was also popular to supply the names of other unnamed disciples. For example, during the same period, we begin to see references to Jesus' maternal grandparents by name, as well as the names of the three wise men. Gnostic portrayals may have provided the impetus to reconsider Mary Magdalene in the New Testament, and the medieval interest in adding details to the Gospels may have provided the methodology to make the connections among Mary of Bethany, the sinful woman, and the woman taken in adultery.

Conclusion

Historically, we know that Mary Magdalene was a close and devoted follower of Jesus Christ. Through an unrecorded miracle, seven evil spirits were cast out of her, which may help explain her profound devotion to the Savior. She followed Him and believed in Him, and somehow she was also able to provide financially for Him. Together with other women disciples, she supported the final years of Jesus' ministry. She may have been a follower of Jesus for the entire three-year ministry, although Luke's account leaves the impression that her financial support of Jesus' ministry may not have lasted much longer than a year. We can reasonably suppose that she supported Jesus from the time she was healed. She was probably a woman of some financial means, and she likely came from Magdala, a significantly important economic center south of Capernaum, on the western shore of the Sea of Galilee.

She loved Jesus, perhaps more than most of the other women disciples. Through grief and emotional pain, she came to the tomb of Jesus to take care of His mortal remains. She had administered to Jesus' temporal needs throughout His ministry, and she continued to do so at the end of His mortal life. Perhaps risking her own life, she overcame any fear of further persecution and visited the tomb—only to find it empty. She remained nearby after all the others had gone. She may even have spent as much as several hours at the tomb before the others left. As a result of her act of devotion and discipleship, the Savior appeared to her while she wept near His empty tomb. Whether out of love, grief, or emotional attachment, she embraced the Savior and thus became the first witness to the physical nature of the Resurrection. She was privileged to become the first to bear witness of the Resurrection. Possessing that personal knowledge of His resurrected reality, she has sometimes been called the "apostle to the Apostles" (see John 20:17).

Later Gnostic traditions build upon this early positive image and make Mary Magdalene a revealer of secret wisdom and knowledge. These later traditions are likely an attempt at filling in the conversation that may have taken place at the empty tomb. They are late and legendary, but to some, they were quite convincing. This legendary literary image of Mary was then used to offer an alternative to apostolic Christian organization and practice, showing the Church leaders how they had erred in suppressing the revelatory knowledge of Mary Magdalene and others.

A consequence of these Gnostic efforts was the medieval suppression of the legends of Mary Magdalene. Rightfully so, the texts that had presented the legendary portrait of Mary were denounced as late forgeries. Rather than clarify who Mary Magdalene really was in the New Testament period, the Church began to merge Mary's identity with that of several other women. This new composite portrait of Mary not only was historically inaccurate but also implied certain things about Mary that were intended to correct the legendary portrait of her. The new, corrected image of Mary gave rise to a cult of Mary as the repentant sinner who came to Jesus in faith. Because the Catholic Church rehabilitated her image for the masses, medieval Christianity saw an increase in depictions of Mary.

By the late Middle Ages, the figure of Mary had been so far removed from her historical roots as to be almost unrecognizable. In 1969, the Catholic Church rescinded the statements made by Pope Gregory I in the sixth century A.D. According to the Vatican statement, Mary Magdalene should no longer be confused with Mary of Bethany, the unnamed sinner of Luke 7, or the woman caught in adultery in John 8.

Centuries of confusion about Mary Magdalene's relationship to other women mentioned in the Gospel accounts have been difficult to erase completely, and, as a result, variant forms of these traditions still persist and crop up from time to time. Recent attention to her in the popular media has only added another layer of tradition, even later than those mentioned in this chapter, obscuring what is clearly known and preserved in the earliest sources—the Gospels themselves. The traditions about Mary Magdalene continued to blossom in the Middle Ages. And legendary reports about her traveling to France, having an interview with the emperor Tiberius, making a trip to Ephesus where she helped John the Apostle write the Gospel of John, and experiencing death near Vézelay at age seventy-two began to surface in the ninth century and later.

Nevertheless, Mary Magdalene is remembered in the canonical Gospels as a member of Jesus' inner circle of disciples. She was present at important and pivotal moments in the story—the Savior's death on the cross, His burial in a rock-hewn tomb outside the city walls, and His appearance at an empty tomb on the first day of the week.

CHAPTER 6

Leonardo's *The Last Supper*

"This fresco, in fact, is the entire key to the Holy Grail mystery.
Da Vinci lays it all out in the open in *The Last Supper.*"

(*The Da Vinci Code,* p. 236)

One of the most poignant stories found in the New Testament
centers around Jesus' last evening among His disciples during His
mortal ministry, known today as the occasion of the "Last
Supper." This dinner is briefly mentioned by Matthew, Mark, and
Luke (Matthew 26:20–30; Mark 14:17–26; Luke 22:14–38).
John, on the other hand, provides a more extended recitation of
what Jesus did and said during this gathering in an upper room in
Jerusalem the night before He died (see John, chapters 13–17).

Interestingly, the earliest account of the Last Supper is not
found in the Gospels but is in Paul's writings. If the books of the
New Testament were printed in the order in which they were originally composed, Paul's letters would appear first. Therefore, his
report, written about A.D. 57 to the Corinthians, most likely pre-
dates any Gospel account: "I have received of the Lord that which
also I delivered unto you, That the Lord Jesus the same night in
which he was betrayed took bread: and when he had given thanks,
he brake it, and said, Take, eat: this is my body, which is broken
for you: this do in remembrance of me. After the same manner
also he took the cup, when he had supped, saying, This cup is the

new testament in my blood: this do ye, as oft as ye drink it, in remembrance of me. For as often as ye eat this bread, and drink this cup, ye do shew the Lord's death till he come" (1 Corinthians 11:23–26).

Undoubtedly, if we had only the words of Paul, our knowledge of the Last Supper would be much more limited. Matthew, Mark, and Luke, authors of the synoptic Gospels, sharing similar material and apparently with the same focus, provide additional information about this gathering: "Now when the even was come, he sat down with the twelve" (Matthew 26:20).

Although the synoptic Gospels differ to some degree in details and language, they basically tell the same story about the Last Supper when Jesus sent at least two disciples to find an upper room for an evening meal (see Mark 14:12–16). John stands apart from these other accounts by preserving significantly more information about what Jesus said and did, but interestingly enough, he did not actually describe the ordinance of the sacrament. However, as in the synoptic Gospels, he does provide us with an account of Jesus' announcement that one of the Twelve will betray Him.

The Synoptics inform us that the disciples sent by Jesus did find a room where they could eat a Passover meal. Later, Jesus came with the Twelve to this room (see Mark 14:17), traditionally identified as the Cenacle and located on Mount Sion in what would have been the upper city of Jerusalem during the first century.

We can assume that the "goodman of the house" and his family members and servants were also present (see Mark 14:14).

The size of the group expands again when we carefully review other details. Luke informs the reader that Jesus "took bread, and gave thanks, and brake it, and gave unto them, saying, This is my body which is given for you: this do in remembrance of me" (Luke 22:19). Luke apparently connects this event with another event reported later in his Gospel and thereby unintentionally provides clues to help us identify others who were present on this momentous night. Luke tells of two disciples, one named Cleopas and the other unnamed, perhaps Cleopas's wife, who were walking from Jerusalem to their home in Emmaus (see Luke 24:13–18). Jesus walked with them, unknown because "their eyes were holden that they should not know him" (Luke 24:16).

When the disciples arrived at their home, they invited Jesus to "Abide with us: for it is toward evening, and the day is far spent" (Luke 24:29). Jesus entered the home and joined them for their evening meal. Luke states, "And it came to pass, as he sat at meat with them, he took bread, and blessed it, and brake, and gave to them" (Luke 24:30). He continued his report: "And their eyes were opened, and they knew him; and he vanished out of their sight" (Luke 24:31). Only later do we find out why they "knew him." The two disciples rushed back to Jerusalem and, upon finding the "eleven gathered together, and them that were with them" (Luke 24:33) in a large upper room (the same room used Thursday evening?), they reported what had happened in their home "And they told what things were done in the way, and how he was known of them in breaking of bread" (Luke 24:35).

Luke suggests, therefore, that these two disciples were also in the upper room and witnessed Jesus institute the sacrament by the taking of the bread, blessing it, breaking it, and giving it to the disciples.

Traditionally, the "large upper room furnished" used on Thursday (see Luke 22:12) has been associated with the room where the disciples, including the eleven, assembled on Sunday (see Luke 24:33); where they gathered with the "women, and Mary the mother of Jesus, and with his brethren" shortly thereafter (Acts 1:14); where a group of 120 gathered on the day Matthias was chosen to replace Judas (see Acts 1:15–26); and where "they were all with one accord" on Pentecost (Acts 2:1). All these events occurred within fifty days of each other in a spacious room that could accommodate a large group of disciples. Additionally, some scholars and readers have also thought the room may be the one alluded to in the first chapters in Acts (see 4:23; 5:6–7, 9–10; 6:2; 11:2; and 12:12), identified with the house of Mary, the mother of Mark, also known as John Mark (Acts 12:12).

We cannot, with any degree of certitude, reconstruct the location or the composition of all the groups involved in these events. However, the evidence does suggest that Jesus met with the Twelve and other disciples on Thursday evening. Those who witnessed the events described by the Gospel may have consisted of the Twelve and other disciples, including the "women that [had] followed him from Galilee" (Luke 23:49). Luke carefully identified the group of women as "Mary Magdalene, and Joanna, and Mary the mother of James, and other women that were with them" (Luke 24:10). These women, Luke tells us, joined Jesus during His ministry in Galilee and "ministered unto him of their substance" (see Luke 8:1–3).

In the end, Jesus likely gathered the Twelve and some of His most intimate disciples, perhaps including women, for a dinner held in a large upper room somewhere in Jerusalem on Thursday evening.

This important gathering has been depicted, based on the written accounts preserved in the New Testament, by almost countless artists over time. Undoubtedly, the most famous rendition is the one by Leonardo da Vinci, *The Last Supper*.

The Last Supper Painting

On the north wall of the refectory (dining hall) of the Convent of Santa Maria delle Grazie in Milan, Italy, Leonardo painted one of the most important and stunning examples of Renaissance art to survive. Leonardo's depiction creates the illusion that Jesus and the Twelve were at the end of the actual

The Last Supper

Detail from *The Last Supper,* 1498, Leonardo da Vinci, Santa Maria delle Grazie, Milan, Italy. This detail highlights three disciples, including John the Beloved, Peter, and Judas, in Leonardo's most famous painting. *Used by Permission, Scala/Art Resource, NY*

dining hall, eating with those present. The painting's beauty results not only from its sublime stylistic features but also, in part, from the execution of the subject matter as well as a break from more traditional depictions. A novel feature of this fresco is that Leonardo did not place Judas on the viewer's side of the table, and this arrangement is a clear break from the traditional organization of the scene that was begun decades earlier in Florence.

According to *The Da Vinci Code,* Leonardo was the head of a secret society known as the Priory of Sion, which had safeguarded some of the world's most important documents from the time of Jesus of Nazareth. These documents purportedly contained information detailing Jesus' marriage to Mary Magdalene and revealed that Leonardo, who was president of the society at one time, brazenly included Mary Magdalene in his portrait of the Last Supper (see *The Da Vinci Code,* pp. 242–43).

Art historians agree that the famous scene depicts Jesus at the very moment He announces that one of the Twelve will betray Him (see Matthew 26:21; Mark 14:18; Luke 22:21; John 13:18). In Leonardo's painting, Jesus is seated with twelve other individuals (in groups of three), who are universally identified as the Twelve Apostles. However, *The Da Vinci Code* suggests that Leonardo painted only eleven of the Twelve and that Mary Magdalene is the twelfth individual in the scene. According to the novel, she is seated to the immediate right of Jesus, who is located in the center of the painting. We must remember that Leonardo himself never provided this interpretation.

To reject the long-standing identification of John the Beloved (the person who would be missing from the painting if *The Da Vinci Code* were correct), we would need access to the same secret documents that Leonardo is reported to have had, or someone who had been granted access to the documents would have to teach us this secret. If such secretive documents were in existence, we would assume they would shed light regarding Mary's presence at the Last Supper as well as on other details. In the absence of such documents, however, we are subjected illogically and unreliably to *The Da Vinci Code*'s imaginative and faulty interpretation of the scene.

This situation is reflective of the major flaw in *The Da Vinci Code*'s historical reconstruction throughout most of the book. The novel provides no evidence except speculation of what might have been. Anyone can claim anything about the past when those from the past are not present to be questioned or interviewed. However, such speculation is often an argument from silence. Therefore, historians must be careful to sift the evidence and then provide probable reconstructions that are based on available evidence. Of course, such a secretive history is alluring, and if and when the facts are revealed, the legend may indeed prove to be more exciting than the reality.

A Brief History of the Painting

Leonardo began his painting of the Last Supper in 1495 as a commissioned work. By the time he had begun painting the scene, he was recognized as one of the most gifted artists of his day. Although much of his work was paid for by Catholic patrons, he seems to have remained relatively aloof from organized religion throughout his life. He completed *The Last Supper* in 1498. According to descriptions, the painting began to crumble almost immediately because of Leonardo's experimental approach in combining water and oil and because of the excessive dampness of the wall on which it was painted. A similar technique was used earlier in Florence, with success, but Milan's notoriously damp air proved devastating to Leonardo's work.

In 1726 (some 228 years after the work had originally been finished), Michelangelo Belloti filled in some of the holes that had developed in the original painting. Using oil paints and varnish, he sought to stabilize the painting from further decay; however, at the same time, he unwittingly initiated the process that would eventually significantly darken the painting and alter the original. Nearly fifty years later, in 1770, Giuseppe Mazza removed Belloti's alterations and repainted ten of the thirteen faces, which were by then beginning to fade. Perhaps the most destructive restoration of the painting took place in 1821, when Stefano Barezzi tried to remove it from the cathedral and restore it at his studio. When he attempted to remove the painting, it cracked in several places, which he reattached to the wall with glue.

In the twentieth century, art conservators began working on the painting again. Following four separate attempts to restore the painting, it was finally returned to public display on 28 May 1999. Unlike the previous attempts to restore the painting, the twentieth-century experts sought to stop the water seepage, clean the painting, and remove the varnish coating that had been added in the eighteenth century. Because the painting was done using a fresco-type technique, some parts of it had to be restored with the use of stucco. The restorations revealed that significant changes to the painting had taken place over the centuries—most notably in facial expressions, gestures, and even the angle of faces and bodies. Using modern methods, art restorers have attempted to peel away these alterations and bring the painting back to its original format and appearance.

When looking at the painting today, visitors are permitted to pass by it briefly. It is displayed under carefully monitored lighting conditions. Although the colors are not as bright today as they were in 1498 when the painting was completed, the modern visitor is presented with what art historians believe is a relatively accurate restoration of what Leonardo originally created.

Even though the painting is over five hundred years old, its history is very well documented, as are the identities of those who worked on it in subsequent centuries.

The Identity of Who Is Depicted in the Painting

The central "evidence" in the declarations of *The Da Vinci Code* is the speculative interpretation given of *The Last Supper*. The novel informs us through one of its fictitional characters that "This fresco, in fact, is the entire key to the Holy Grail mystery. Da Vinci lays it all out in the open in *The Last Supper*" (*The Da Vinci Code*, p. 236). To get the reader ready to accept this revision interpretation, *The Da Vinci Code* must paint a word-picture—provide a pair of new lenses to see the painting as we have not seen it before. In the end, this pair of lenses does not bring anything into focus but ultimately only blurs the reader's vision of this wonderful painting, which highlights the pathos of the poignant moment when Jesus announces that "One of you which eateth with me shall betray me" (Mark 14:18).

The Da Vinci Code tells us that "In the painting, Peter was leaning menacingly toward Mary Magdalene and slicing his blade-like hand across her neck" (*The Da Vinci Code,* p. 248). Now that the author has prepared the reader to see as he interprets the scene, he then continues through sheer fabrication to add an additional witness that his interpretation is correct. We are informed that Peter's gesture is the "same threatening gesture as in *Madonna of the Rocks*!" (*The Da Vinci Code,* p. 248). What *The Da Vinci Code* evidently counts on is that the average reader will not be familiar with Leonardo's other referenced work, *Madonna of the Rocks.*

Two versions of the work exist. The first is found in the Musée du Louvre in Paris, and the second is found in the National Gallery in London. While in Milan, Leonardo painted the *Virgin of the Rocks* (known also as the *Madonna of the Rocks*) in about 1485. The paintings, though slightly different, depict four individuals—the Virgin Mary (the Madonna), the infant Jesus, the infant John the Baptist, and an angel. In the one version, housed in the Louvre, the "same threatening gesture" is actually the hand of the angel pointing toward John the Baptist who is praying to Jesus, who responds by blessing John. For those unfamiliar with this painting, it is important also to note that Peter and Mary Magdalene are not depicted in the scene; therefore, the painting has absolutely nothing to do with *The Last Supper.*

The Da Vinci Code continues this interpretation, suggesting that all the disciples are depicted with the same malevolence toward Mary Magdalene that Peter's character expresses. "A bit ominous, no?" Robert Langdon asks (*The Da Vinci Code,* p. 248). The novel continues by depicting this violent moment: "Sophie squinted and saw a hand emerging from the crowd of disciples. 'Is that hand wielding a *dagger?*' 'Yes. Stranger still, if you count the arms, you'll see that this hand belongs to . . . no one at all. It's disembodied. Anonymous'" (*The Da Vinci Code,* p. 248). Now readers are ready to see exactly what *The Da Vinci Code* wants them to see—completely turning the standard interpretation upside down.

Among the most important sources used during the recent twenty-year-long restoration of *The Last Supper* were Leonardo's notebooks, studies, and surviving sketches for the painting. In addition, fifteenth-century traditions of depictions of this scene by other masters and painters as well as copies of the painting completed in the sixteenth century provide valuable insights regarding the identification of those depicted in the Milan fresco. Unfortunately, *The Da Vinci Code* conveniently neglects this extensive evidence. Leonardo's notebooks, sketches, and studies for *The Last Supper* are found in the Royal Library at Windsor Castle in Berkshire, England, and in the Galleria dell'Accademia in Venice, Italy. An important copy of the painting, one that contains the names of the Twelve, is found in the Chiesa di Sant'Ambrogio at Ponte Capriaca (Lugano), Switzerland.

None of the traditions for depicting this scene from the fifteenth century; none of the surviving notebooks, studies, and sketches prepared by Leonardo for the painting; and none of the copies made of Leonardo's painting in the sixteenth century contain any hint or allusion that the figure seated next to Christ is a woman. They all indicate with near certainty that it is John who is depicted seated on Jesus' right hand. As in other paintings of the Last Supper, Leonardo depicts Peter beckoning to John, soliciting him to ask Jesus who it is who would betray Him (see John 13:21–25).

The real danger, both in terms of providing accurate historical details for this murder-mystery and the kind of thought processes that such a historical novel induces, is *The Da Vinci Code*'s uniquely outlandish idea about something art historians universally agree upon. The novel's bizarre interpretation is a blatantly apparent effort to misrepresent, distort, and completely fabricate the past.

What is certain is that we cannot accept the possibility that anyone can simply look at the painting and offer his or her own conjecture without some controls because, on certain points, we have no way to prove or disprove a speculative interpretation. We must assess what are the historical probabilities, given the data at hand. In this case, we do have the canonical texts—the Gospels themselves. With these texts, an artist can legitimately take only certain liberties because the texts provide the governing control of the story.

For instance, if we were to commission a painting of Jesus in Gethsemane, we would be controlled by the text because it is the only evidence of what happened there. According to the account preserved in Mark, the earliest existing account of the moment, Jesus took three disciples (Peter, James, and John) with Him as He moved further into the shadows of the olive grove (see Mark 14:33). He then went a little distance from them and began to pray (see Mark 14:35). Because the text is all we have, an artist is bound by some of the data preserved in the primary source; thus, depicting the scene with Jesus praying and with three disciples nearby is appropriate. What would be inappropriate is for some person to identify the four individuals depicted in the scene as Jesus, James, John, and the unknown young man mentioned in the story (see Mark 14:51–52). If such a scene were composed by a painter, it would be natural for someone to ask about Peter, "Where is he?"

The same rationale holds true of the events of the Last Supper. We have a recognized canon of individuals who attended the Last Supper meal—the Twelve Apostles and Jesus. An artist may add servants and others who may have joined the Twelve with Jesus on this evening, as noted above, but the Twelve and Jesus are fixed and static. Without question, we know they were there.

If *The Da Vinci Code* is right in its unbridled speculation, how can we account for the absence of John the Beloved? How do we explain the presence of only eleven of the Twelve? These seem to be insurmountable problems that *The Da Vinci Code* does not address adequately and, in some cases, not at all.

Therefore, if *The Last Supper* were to present Jesus sitting next to Mary Magdalene, then it would be the first surviving painting to do so. Certainly we can look at it and suggest that John the Beloved looks overly feminine or that his shoulders are not as masculine as those of the other figures in this work. We can also look at Leonardo's preparatory drawings of other Apostles for his painting that reflect even more femininity, but nothing has ever been said about them. In fact, art historians have noted that artists of this period commonly portrayed young men in this manner. In particular, there are many examples in which John is depicted as being young, beardless, and slender and having long hair and soft features.

Most importantly, without some external confirmation, *The Da Vinci Code*'s thesis about John the Beloved must remain only a hypothetical conjecture. Some historians have argued that the depiction of John the Beloved has not fared as well in the restorations of the painting as other depictions have, but no one else has suggested that the person we thought was John was really Mary Magdalene. The most recent restoration also shows very liberal repainting of facial types, gestures, and so forth over the centuries that grossly changed Leonardo's composition.

The Impact of *The Da Vinci Code*'s Hypothesis

One positive result of *The Da Vinci Code*'s sensational and speculative interpretation of the Last Supper is that it has created an interest in Renaissance art, some of the best art ever created. Leonardo's painting, which was already an icon being reproduced on items as diverse as mouse pads and T-shirts, has recently graced the covers of books, including this one, and has been included in chapters of other books and printed with articles in the wake of numerous attempts to respond to *The Da Vinci Code*. This outcome may not be at all bad.

However, another result that is far less positive as an outgrowth from *The Da Vinci Code*'s controversial interpretation of Leonardo's famous painting is that this kind of approach at reconstructing the past, even in a novel that claims to be well researched, ultimately dulls our ability to think critically about revisionist interpretations of history. Tools that encourage both an openness to the past and respectful questioning have been thrown out the proverbial window as we have become engrossed in a fast-paced drama in a modern setting—but with a purported background of historical reliability.

Most of all, in *The Da Vinci Code*'s thoroughly unhistorical approach in a historical novel, the book's dogmatic assertion that "all descriptions of artwork, architecture, documents, and secret rituals . . . are accurate" (*The Da Vinci Code*, p. 1) does more to confuse than to clarify. In the end, *The Last Supper* does not hold the most shocking and amazing coded secrets of all time and is certainly not "one of the most astonishing tributes to the sacred feminine you will ever see" (*The Da Vinci Code*, p. 96).

Finally, even if the slightest possibility exists that *The Da Vinci Code* is right in its quirky interpretation of Leonardo's painting of this poignant scene, we cannot forget that Leonardo himself was far removed, by time and space, from the event he depicts. No other reliable documents beyond the New Testament are available to provide us any information whatever regarding the events that took place in an upper room in Jerusalem in A.D. 30.

CHAPTER 7

Women in Early Christianity

"Sophie looked at him. 'You're saying the Christian
Church was to be carried on by a *woman*?' 'That was the plan. Jesus
was the original feminist. He intended for the future of His Church
to be in the hands of Mary Magdalene.'"

(*The Da Vinci Code,* p. 248)

Two of the main characters in *The Da Vinci Code* are Sophie
Neveu and Sir Leigh Teabing. Sophie represents the millions
of readers who, like her, are supposedly moving out from the
shadows of their current misunderstanding of the past into the
light of an old and "hidden" truth. In this journey of discovery,
Teabing is her guide, as *The Da Vinci Code* is the reader's guide,
through the mists of the "suppressed past" into the "brightness of
noonday."

In a provocative "revelation" in the novel, the reader discovers
that the Catholic Church has suppressed the sacred feminine manifested in ancient goddess worship that was originally part of the
biblical record. Further, as we learn from a conversation between
Sophie and Teabing, this was part of a larger and more compli-
cated conspiracy.

In the resulting dialogue, Teabing informs Sophie that Peter
was jealous of Mary Magdalene. Sophie innocently asks, "Because
Jesus preferred Mary?" Of course, what we are about to be told is
not only that Peter was jealous but also that "the stakes were far
greater than mere affection" (*The Da Vinci Code,* p. 247).

95

Fresco of Woman
Lunette with Orante Fresco, third century A.D., Catacomb of Priscilla, Rome, Italy.
This fresco shows a woman with outstretched arms praying and is one of the earliest
depictions of a Christian woman. *Used by Permission, Scala/Art Resource, NY*

The bombshell follows: "At this point in the gospels, Jesus suspects He will soon be captured and crucified. So He gives Mary Magdalene instructions on how to carry on His Church after He is gone. As a result, Peter expresses his discontent over playing second fiddle to a woman" (*The Da Vinci Code*, pp. 247–48).

So, according to *The Da Vinci Code*'s reconstruction of history, Jesus wanted Mary to lead the Church instead of Peter. The book claims, through the voices of its fictional characters, that this can be proven from the earliest Christian documents—the Nag Hammadi codices. Ultimately, the novel claims not only that the New Testament presents a later alternative to this more authentic truth but also that the New Testament represents a false gospel that is not "good news" after all.

A New Synthesis

The *Da Vinci Code* either is confused or purposely misuses historical sources to provide a radical revisionist view of the past. Many of the faithful will be willing to dismiss this perspective as utter nonsense, unworthy of any response. However, we would be missing the point if we accepted that stance without comment. *The Da Vinci Code* has not provided us a simple story for entertainment purposes only but has tapped into recent phenomena in Western culture. There are voices among us who are attempting to reinvent our culture by substituting the long-standing traditional Judeo-Christian culture and character with one that is fundamentally different, though the trappings are still present.

Likely, many of these modern voices have been personally marginalized by Christians and Christianity and have sought an alternative home wherein they could freely express their religious understanding. Other voices may have described directly or indirectly the general collapse of traditional social, religious, and moral structures, allowing a kind of radical individualism to become an official dogmatic religion. The result of either or the combination of both has been to replace the core message of the New Testament with a blend of various and often conflicting and contradictory visions of ancient spirituality.

Many of the themes in *The Da Vinci Code* simply reflect and, in some cases, borrow directly from scholarly attempts to reconstruct the past in a convoluted potage of rejected pagan beliefs, discarded Gnostic practices, and medieval legends.

In the end, *The Da Vinci Code* argues that early Christianity focused attention on the sacred feminine, a concept that was only later suppressed by the Catholic Church. The book contends that this original Christian view has been kept vouchsafed by the secretive Priory of Sion: "The Priory believes that Constantine and his male successors successfully converted the world from matriarchal paganism to patriarchal Christianity by waging a campaign of propaganda that demonized the sacred feminine, obliterating the goddess from modern religion forever" (*The Da Vinci Code,* p. 124).

The Gnostic Connection

As noted earlier, *The Da Vinci Code* argues, without basis, that the Nag Hammadi codices preserve the earliest written account of Christianity, the "unaltered gospel," and, if read carefully, reveal the prominent and significant role women played in the earliest strata of Christian tradition. Additionally, *The Da Vinci Code* cites another Gnostic gospel, the *Gospel of Mary,* discovered in Egypt at the turn of the century, to help buttress the novel's contentions.

Scholars have shown that Gnosticism was not a monolithic religious system but rather consisted of diverse beliefs and practices. In other words, Gnosticism was historically a parasitic religious movement. Gnosticism existed initially through negative definition, declaring itself unique from the orthodox faith in specific ways. Only later did Gnosticism develop its own complex set of beliefs and practices. *The Da Vinci Code*'s characters oversimplify this diversity of thought and, in many cases, distort the evidence to fit a view that even many Gnostics would not recognize or would reject.

For example, in one of the arguments used to prove this revisionist interpretation, *The Da Vinci Code* offers grossly exaggerated claims about the number of supporting points that could be mustered to prove this theory (countless modern historians) and then falsifies the one text the author uses to prove his point: "Sir Leigh Teabing was still talking. 'I shan't bore you with the countless references to Jesus and Magdalene's union. That has been explored ad nauseam by modern historians. I would, however, like to point out the following.' He motioned to another passage. 'This is from the Gospel of Mary Magdalene'" (*The Da Vinci Code*, p. 247).

Like countless readers of *The Da Vinci Code*, Sophie had not heard that Mary's words had supposedly been preserved in a "gospel." Without any evaluation, the reader is to assume, as Sophie does, that this gospel is equal to or even superior to the Gospels of Matthew, Mark, Luke, or John found in the New Testament.

The narrative continues: "She read the text: *And Peter said, 'Did the Saviour really speak with a woman without our knowledge? Are we to turn about and all listen to her? Did he prefer her to us?' And Levi answered, 'Peter, you have always been hot-tempered. Now I see you contending against the woman like an adversary. If the Saviour made her worthy, who are you indeed to reject her? Surely the Saviour knows her very well. That is why he loved her more than us'"* (*The Da Vinci Code*, p. 247; italics in original).

For those who are careful readers, this dialogue is full of contradictions as well as irony. Earlier, *The Da Vinci Code* claims the earliest Christians did not accept Jesus as divine. However, when the book needs to prove that the earliest Christians celebrated the sacred feminine, it quotes from a text that not only declares but also celebrates Jesus' divine nature. (Note that Jesus is called "Saviour" in this passage.)

The Da Vinci Code's claim that this conversation occurred before Jesus' death and that it centers on who will lead the Church is blatantly false. To be sure, Mary holds an important role in this severely damaged text, dated between the mid-second and mid-third century. However, the emphasis is not on leading the Church but on obtaining personal salvation and definitely is a post-resurrection experience. (Note again that Jesus is resurrected and is thus divine.)

The text was of interest to Gnostics because the issue raised is whether a vision given to a woman could be trusted. Apparently, some Gnostics argued that a woman could be a vehicle for divine knowledge, whereas other Gnostics rejected such a proposal. As in other Gnostic documents, the author's attitude here about women is less than ideal. Generally, the Gnostic world is one of radical asceticism composed completely and unequivocally of ardent misogynistic attitudes, beliefs, and practices. Indeed, one strain of Gnostic belief argued that only men could be saved and that, more important to our discussion, the feminine nature had to be totally destroyed for a person to be redeemed. That is not quite the rosy picture of the favored status of women presented by *The Da Vinci Code* about the Gnostics.

The Larger Context

To place in proper context the earliest Christian view of women, that found in the New Testament, we must understand some general attitudes of the larger non-Jewish culture of the period.

Almost without exception, the general pattern throughout the classical age was of the political, legal, economic, and social subordination of women to men. On the whole, this distinction between the private affairs of the woman in the home and the public concerns of the man outside was also maintained in Roman life during the Republic, the time shortly before Jesus and His Apostles. Any threat to dissolve or reorient the boundaries was seen by men as a surreptitious threat to the stability of the society.

Not until the late Republic and early Empire periods were certain aristocratic women found in the center stage of the public arena of Roman life. During this period, privileged women began to experience social change that manifested itself in many different forms. There was a tendency, for example, for the free woman to throw off her veil, when the accepted custom was for her to appear veiled in public.

However, the advancement made by some women in individual worth and identity during this period was made possible by the status of the men to whom the women had connection (fathers, husbands, or sons). When women were recognized in inscriptions recording benefaction or receipts of a civil largesse or when a statue was erected in honor of a woman, it was largely because of matrimonial relations.

Generally, scholars suggest that in the Greco-Roman world, a broad division existed between the public and private spheres of daily life. The former was an inappropriate sphere for a woman. Her domain was the private confines of the home. In the home, she clearly exercised greater freedom. Basically, only in the upper classes was there any deviation from the generally accepted ideals and practices of what women should and should not do. In the end, even the women from the upper classes were expected to perform duties relegated to lower-class women—spinning and weaving.

New Testament Window

As we have demonstrated earlier, the New Testament is a useful source to help us reconstruct early Christian views, thoughts, and practices. The twenty-seven texts that compose the New

Testament provide a remarkable amount of data that can give a rather detailed description of the role and status of women in the first-century Church.

Fifty-one different women, though some are from the Old Testament, are named in the New Testament. Obviously, the number of women assumed to be present in any setting is significantly larger than the identifiable group of individual women who are named. Modern translations struggle to use gender-inclusive language to reveal women's presence. However, translators are confronted with a difficult challenge of knowing when New Testament writers may have envisioned both males and females as part of their audience. Certainly, it is inconceivable to imagine that any of the writers of the New Testament envisioned their respective audiences (except where a book was specifically sent to an individual) as wholly made up of men or that their instructions or teachings were limited only to men.

A significant amount of information about women in the New Testament can be gleaned from the writings of Luke (the Gospel of Luke and Acts) and Paul's epistle to the Romans.

Luke's Account

In the Gospel of Luke, Jesus is portrayed as solicitous to and encouraging of women. Women are highlighted as active participants in Jesus' message, healing ministry, and mission. His teachings, in many respects, stood apart from the prevailing attitudes toward women in the larger Greco-Roman society and the Jewish subculture within it. Unlike women in the Old Testament, such as Eve, Sarah, Rebekah, Leah, and Rachel, women in the New Testament are surprisingly visible. Their presence in Luke is specifically highlighted.

First, Luke introduces us to Mary, the mother of Jesus (see Luke 1:26–56). Unlike other women of the period, whose positions were primarily based on who their father was, who their husband was, and who their sons were, Mary's role as the "highly favored" one is the basis for our viewing her as a disciple who hears and responds to God's word (see Luke 1:28).

Luke also highlights certain women "which ministered unto [Jesus] of their substance" (Luke 8:3). These women—Mary Magdalene, Joanna, Susanna, and others—traveled with Jesus and the disciples throughout Galilee. At the end of Luke's account, they reappear in Jerusalem at the cross, the burial, and the empty tomb (Luke 23:49, 55; 24:1, 10). In this they play a significant and vital role as witnesses of all three events: the death, burial, and resurrection of Christ. In fact, the presence of women in all four Gospels is very remarkable, particularly in the Passion and Resurrection narratives—the heart of the Gospels.

We are left, after a careful reading of Luke, with the clear impression that, to Jesus, the intrinsic value of women is equal to that of men—an idea found nowhere else in the society of Jesus' day. This attitude reveals drastic differences between the ways Jesus and society treated women and also clearly demonstrates how He expected his male disciples to treat women.

Luke highlights Jesus' sensitivities to individuals, especially those whom society has marginalized or relegated to the fringes; he shows this clearly in Jesus' speeches and actions. Jesus treated women as valued individuals. It is not so much that He attempted to raise women to the level of men, for He did not appear to view people as being on differing levels, but rather that He saw men and women as persons—as responsible individuals with individual needs, individual failings, and individual talents. Jesus gave very few teachings on women as a group because He never treated them as a separate class with clone-like characteristics and tendencies. Similarly, He gave very few teachings for or about males as a distinct group. Luke reveals Jesus' attitudes toward discipleship in general—not His views on the specifics of male or female discipleship.

As Luke continues his story in the book of Acts, women are frequently highlighted, and their roles are identified as supporters, leaders, and benefactors of the teachings and ministries of the Apostles of Jesus.

During his transition from his gospel narrative to the book of Acts, Luke reports that the disciples gathered in an upper room in Jerusalem, "where abode both Peter, and James, and John, and Andrew, Philip, and Thomas, Bartholomew, and Matthew, James the son of Alphaeus, and Simon Zelotes, and Judas the brother of James" (Acts 1:13). Luke then states, "These all continued with one accord in prayer and supplication, with the women, and Mary the mother of Jesus, and with his brethren" (Acts 1:14).

As Luke narrates the persecution that followed the disciples, he informs the reader that Paul, known as Saul at the time, "made havock of the church, entering into every house, and haling men and women committed them to prison" (Acts 8:3). Obviously, Luke wants us to know that women constituted an important part of the early Church, one that persecuters would not overlook.

Luke tells us that the disciples of Jesus, as Jesus had done, continued to reach out to women in their healing ministry (see Acts 9:36–42). They also provided assistance to the early missionaries, just as women had done for Jesus' own mission. For example, Lydia hosted a Christian house-church (see Acts 16:14–15). At other times, women became important co-laborers, teaching and preaching the gospel to others (see Acts 18:24–26).

The Book of Romans

A boon for New Testament scholars and germane to our interests, Romans 16 provides a wealth of information about the early Christians. The material, identified as the "Greeting Chapter," reveals not only diversity in ethnic origin and social status but also diversity in gender in the early Christian congregations in Rome. Of the twenty-nine individuals mentioned, ten are women: Phebe,

Priscilla, Mary, Junia, Tryphena, Tryphosa, Persis, the mother of Rufus, Julia, and the sister of Nereus.

Romans 16 also reveals additional information not found elsewhere in the New Testament about the status of women in the early Christian congregations. In particular, more women than men received praise for being especially active in the Church. Some of the women who are specifically named are: Priscilla, Mary, Junia, Tryphena, Tryphosa, Persis, and Rufus's mother. Paul provides important clues about their labors for the ministry when he identifies Phebe as "a servant of the church which is at Cenchrea" and one who has "been a succourer of many, and of myself also" (Romans 16:1–2); Priscilla, who along with her husband, "have for my life laid down their own necks" (Romans 16:4); Mary, "who bestowed much labour on us" (Romans 16:6); Junia, a fellow Jew, who had been a prisoner for Christ's sake and was "of note among the apostles" (Romans 16:7); Tryphena and Tryphosa, "who labour in the Lord" (Romans 16:12); Persis, "which laboured much in the Lord" (Romans 16:12); and finally Rufus's mother, who was "chosen in the Lord," suggesting some type of spiritual guide or nurturer instead of a biological relationship (see Romans 16:13).

Clearly, women joined men in almost every aspect of Christian ministry, including missionary labors.

Conclusion

The earliest and most reliable Christian documents, the books of the New Testament, provide a clear view of Jesus' attitudes about women and their roles in the earliest congregations of the Church. In what may be the earliest document in the New Testament, dated about A.D. 49, Paul reports: "There is neither Jew nor Greek, there is neither bond nor free, there is neither male nor female: for ye are all one in Christ Jesus" (Galatians 3:28). This verse may be the clearest statement of women's equity to be found in the New Testament. It appears that Galatians 3:28 is not an original composition of Paul but is the quotation by him of a saying associated with the ordinance of baptism or teachings about it, presumably taught and recognized by the early Christian communities. If so, the declaration would date to even earlier than A.D. 49.

The earliest Christians believed this hope was not just to be suddenly realized in the future but also a reality to be experienced in the present. Through baptism, their congregations were often demarcated from the larger society whose social inequality and hierarchies of race, class, and gender were contradictory to Jesus' teachings. The implications of Galatians 3:28 for gender roles and status are monumental, considering how the abolition of these social hierarchies would promote greater equality.

The favorable status of women in the early Christian Church has been long recognized. It was recognized as such by both the early Christian writers and their opponents. When the pagan critic Celsus denigrated Christianity in the second century as a religion of women, children, and slaves, he may have meant to confirm what elite, educated men in the Greco-Roman world already believed: any religion that appealed to women was the wrong sort of religion. But in reality he was articulating a connection between women and early Christianity that has only recently recieved serious attention.

The message of Jesus and those who followed after Him in the wake of His suffering, death, and resurrection was profoundly and radically challenging to Greco-Roman and Jewish sensibilities, values, and ideals. For Jesus, marriage was sacred. Yet divorce was common and had been allowed since the moorings of Greco-Roman culture were established. Another principle that Jesus preached that Romans found disturbing was that men and women had equal dignity in marriage. That these fundamental ideas contributed no small amount to giving Christian women a new consciousness and to teaching Christian men greater respect for women is beyond dispute. As a result, men and women were more equally yoked, giving both added purpose in life and added happiness in its living.

Ironically, *The Da Vinci Code*'s argument for the superiority of women in the first century derives from sources that actually view women in a less than positive light, contradictory to the novel's reconstruction of them. Many readers do not realize that the texts used in *The Da Vinci Code* to support the existence of a cult of the sacred feminine in reality advocate radical celibacy and androgyny. If women are in any way elevated in these Gnostic texts, then it is an elevation to a state of "heavenly androgyny" where men and women live eternally without gender. This is hardly what *The Da Vinci Code* has in mind when it refers to these early texts. The great irony is that the Gnostic texts themselves are not as liberal in their views toward women as the canonical texts are. If *The Da Vinci Code* did have one point right, then, it is that Jesus was inclusive in His teachings toward all women and men. But His teachings are more accurately represented in the Gospels and not in hidden or esoteric Gnostic texts.

Conclusion

"Religious allegory has become a part of the
fabric of reality. And living in that reality helps millions of
people cope and be better people."

(*The Da Vinci Code*, p. 342)

The Da Vinci Code is certainly a fascinating and entertaining
read, although some individuals question whether the reading
public might be taking the novel too seriously. A way around this
concern has been to point to the fact that as a result of the popularity of *The Da Vinci Code*, millions of people who would otherwise be unknowledgeable are now somewhat familiar with the
Nag Hammadi codices, the *Gospel of Philip*, the *Gospel of Mary*,
other early Gnostic texts, and important works of art such as
Leonardo da Vinci's painting *The Last Supper*. Further, New
Testament scholars have lamented for decades that the Dead Sea
Scrolls have overshadowed the Nag Hammadi texts, even though
the latter are far more important for the study of Christianity.
Because *The Da Vinci Code* has increased public interest in the
subject of the origins of Christianity and has made millions aware
of the Nag Hammadi texts, we owe the novel our thanks.

At the same time, the book begins with the bold and stunning
false statement that "All descriptions of artwork, architecture, documents, and secret rituals in this novel are accurate" (*The Da Vinci
Code*, p. 1). Was this statement included to add intrigue to a

well-written novel, or was it intended as a statement of the author's beliefs that what he presents is accurate? The answer to this question has far-reaching consequences for our understanding of Christianity.

At the very heart of the matter are questions about the origins of Christianity and about who Jesus really was. What *The Da Vinci Code* has achieved, more than any serious scholarly work has achieved, is to popularize liberal scholarship. With the exception of the hypothesis that Jesus was married to Mary Magdalene, liberal scholars have for decades been advocating nearly every one of the claims made in this novel about Jesus of Nazareth. From the early dating of Gnostic texts to the period before the written Gospels to the claim that Jesus' followers did not believe that He was a God, these positions have all been discussed fully in academic journals and at scholarly conferences. The difference between those discussions and *The Da Vinci Code*'s presentation and manipulation of them is that the novel has popularized them in a way that has made the subject palatable for everyday people.

From a scholarly standpoint, what has been the most interesting observation is that the novel has drawn the attention of both liberal and conservative scholars from all Christian denominations. We might assume that liberal scholars would be happy to have their theories advanced in a popular format and that conservative scholars would decry the inaccuracies in the novel. Surprisingly, these outcomes are not the case. Both liberal and conservative scholars have denounced the inaccuracies in the novel with equal fervor. For example, some of the best-recognized names in the field of New Testament studies—such as Bart D. Ehrman, more liberal, and Ben Witherington III, more conservative—have joined in the fray against *The Da Vinci Code*. Both of these scholars, who come from starkly diverse backgrounds, have written books to identify the errors in the novel. And even though many scholars would be happy to see the history of Christianity rewritten in a way envisioned in *The Da Vinci Code,* no academic appreciates the process of doing so through faulty logic and scholarship as found in that book.

Apart from the intriguing murder mystery that is the focus of the novel, the following doctrines are attacked in the book:

1. The divinity of Jesus Christ.

2. Christ's role as Savior and Redeemer of mankind.

3. The legitimacy of the early Christian Church.

4. The integrity of our canonical New Testament.

5. The very existence of God the Father and His Son, Jesus Christ.

6. The commandment of chastity.

7. The authority of the original Quorum of Twelve Apostles.

Perhaps it could be said that we have taken such issues all too seriously, and perhaps we should dismiss it as simply an interesting novel that happens to treat sacred subjects in a popular way. At the same time, however, the subject is of eternal consequence.

As scholars of religious education, we immediately noticed the dramatic, unsupported claims in the novel. We easily discerned the surprising manipulation of scholarly positions. At first we thought that our talk on CD ("What Da Vinci Didn't Know: LDS Perspectives on the *Code,*" Deseret Book, 2005) would be a helpful way to differentiate facts from fiction. But since then each of us has been contacted by various individuals who wanted more details about the subject in a more direct approach. Other prominent scholars have written on the subject and, although each of them deals with only a few of the questions of the book, we initially thought that other scholarly discussions could answer the many questions and concerns that were being raised.

More recently, however, the media have caught on to the ideas presented in the novel and are passing off those ideas as if they were truths. Major television and cable networks have scrambled to produce special segments devoted to exploring early

Christianity and have inquired whether *The Da Vinci Code* presents an accurate portrait of the facts. Increasingly, the public is being fed the ideas that "that is how it was" and "you are going to have to learn to cope with it."

Some of those trying to find their way through these productions may be surprised to learn that it was *not* that way. Jesus' followers loved Him and worshipped Him even during His mortal life, and a small group of those followers held tenaciously, even after His death, to the Church He had organized in His name. They preserved His teachings and believed that what He taught them was authoritative enough to cause them to leave behind their ancestral religion—Judaism—and begin living the gospel He had taught them. They left everything behind for the truths He taught because they were persuaded He had redeemed them, and they were eternally grateful to Him for the love He had shown them. He appeared as a man, but He was and is God.

What many people also fail to grasp is the simple fact that even if someone in the first century believed and wrote that Jesus married Mary Magdalene, that He was only a mortal man, or that Mary was destined to lead a feminist movement in His honor, such thinking does not create reality. Someone may have thought those ideas—although we have absolutely no surviving evidence that anyone did—but if they did, their thinking does not qualify as truth.

Another especially important question also looms large in the background—one for which there is probably no accurate answer. The question is whether the novel has satisfied the thirst of a liberal minority who have become dissatisfied with traditional forms of Christianity. All across the nation, Christianity is under an increasingly careful and nuanced attack from its more liberal adherents. Initially, because Jesus' life has traditionally been the focus of the gospel, this attack has centered on rewriting the history of His life in a way that permits more liberal beliefs and practices. The logic is that if liberals could prove that certain ideas and

Early Depiction of Christ
The Good Shepherd Fresco, early third century A.D., Catacomb of San Callisto, Rome, Italy. Frescoes such as this one show that Christians believed in Jesus' divinity. Jesus depicted as the Good Shepherd is one of the most common themes in early Christian art. *Used by Permission, Scala/Art Resource, NY*

practices existed in the Bible or among members of the New Testament Church, then those same ideas and practices should be part of Christian practice today.

In the last few years, these same liberal advocates have moved Jesus from being the *center* of importance to being merely an important *part of* Christianity. According to some Christians, He was an inspiring man—but not the Savior of the world. The most recent trend has been to create an ethical system that mirrors Christianity's ethics without Jesus' saving acts at the center. Like the teachings of other great prophets and moral men, Jesus' teachings are regarded as important—but only inasmuch as He saved Himself from the corruption of this world. Many individuals would be surprised to realize that *The Da Vinci Code* taps into the core beliefs of these liberal Christians and presents them with surprising clarity and force. Maybe this novel is indeed an "innocent" presentation. What is of greatest concern, however, is that the novel has also captured the attention of conservative Christians who are equally drawn to its teachings.

We hope, more than anything else, that our discussions of some of the most salient issues raised in the novel will be helpful to those who have wanted to know more. Like other readers, we enjoyed the suspense of the novel, and we appreciated the complex character development and the intricately woven plot. We have been concerned about the popular treatment of sacred subjects, and so we have attempted to present the reader with careful historical analysis. We leave it to the reader to decide whether the claim presented in the novel that "all descriptions of artwork, architecture, documents, and secret rituals . . . are accurate" (*The Da Vinci Code,* p. 1) is intended as dramatic flair to heighten the suspense or whether this is an attempt at genuine revisionist Christian history. Indeed, each of us is an advocate of Teabing's inclination: "Learning the truth has become my life's love" (*The Da Vinci Code,* p. 242). But we also encourage readers of *The Da Vinci Code* to remember that there are good reasons the book is called fiction!

Notes

Notes to Chapter 2

1. Translated in William Whiston, *The Works of Josephus* (Peabody, MA: Hendrickson, 1987).

2. Whiston, *The Works of Josephus.*

3. Translated in John Jackson, *Tacitus: Annals XIII-XVI* (Cambridge, MA: Loeb Classical Library 322, Harvard University, 1991).

4. Translated in J. C. Rolfe, Suetonius, *The Lives of the Caesars,* 2 vols. (Cambridge, MA: Harvard Press, 1970).

5. Translated in Alexander Roberts and James Donaldson, eds., *Ante-Nicene Fathers,* 10 vols. (Peabody, MA: Hendrickson, 1999), 1:8.

6. Roberts and Donaldson, Ante-Nicene Fathers, 1:87.

7. Translated in John S. Kloppenborg, Marvin W. Meyer, Stephen J. Patterson, and Michael G. Steinhauser, *Q Thomas Reader* (Sonoma, CA: Polebridge Press, 1990), 147.

8. Translated in Ron Cameron, ed., *The Other Gospels: Non-Canonical Gospel Texts* (Philadelphia: Westminster Press, 1982), 54.

9. Translated in James M. Robinson, ed., *The Nag Hammadi Library,* rev. ed. (New York: HarperSanFrancisco, 1988), 525.

Notes to Chapter 3

1. "The Gospel of Philip," introduced and translated by Wesley W. Isenberg, in *The Nag Hammadi Library,* general editor James M. Robinson

(San Francisco: Harper and Row, 1977), 138. The diacritic markings indicating line-breaks have been removed for ease of reading.

2. "Gospel of Philip," 138.

3. "Gospel of Philip," 2.

4. "Gospel of Philip," 131.

5. See Joseph Smith, *Teachings of the Prophet Joseph Smith,* sel. Joseph Fielding Smith (Salt Lake City: Deseret Book, 1972), 308; Joseph F. Smith, "Discources of Joseph F. Smith," *Millennial Star* 62 (February 15, 1900), 97.

6. Scott G. Kenny, ed., *Wilford Woodruff's Journal: 1833–1898 Typescript* (July 22, 1883), 8:187–88; *Wilford Woodruff's Journal* (February 8, 1841), 2:79–82.

7. Charles W. Penrose, "Editor's Table," *Improvement Era* 15:11 (September 1912): 1042.

8. Joseph B. Wirthlin, "Deep Roots." *Ensign* (November 1994), 77.

Notes to Chapter 5

1. Translated in James M. Robinson, *The Nag Hammadi Library* (New York: HarperSanFrancisco, 1990), 526.

2. Robinson, *The Nag Hammadi Library,* 527.

3. Robinson, *The Nag Hammadi Library,* 148.

4. Translated in John S. Kloppenborg, Marvin W. Meyer, Stephen J. Patterson, and Michael G. Steinhauser, *Q Thomas Reader* (Sonoma, CA: Polebridge Press, 1990), 154.

5. Translated in Wilhelm Schneemelcher, *New Testament Apocrypha,* trans. R. McL. Wilson, 2 vols. (Louisville: Westminster/John Knox Press, 1991), 1:254-55.

6. Schneemelcher, *New Testament Apocrypha,* 1:225.

Bibliography

Aland, Kurt, and Barbara Aland. *The Text of the New Testament: An Introduction to the Critical Editions and to the Theory and Practice of Modern Textual Criticism.* 2d ed., rev. and enlarged. Translated Erroll F. Rhodes. Grand Rapids: W. B. Eerdmans; Leiden: E.J. Brill, 1989.

Bock, Darrell L. *Breaking the Da Vinci Code: Answers to the Questions Everyone's Asking.* Nashville: Nelson, 2004.

Ehrman, Bart D. *Truth and Fiction in The Da Vinci Code: A Historian Reveals What We Really Know about Jesus, Mary Magdalene, and Constantine.* Oxford: Oxford University Press, 2004.

Jung, Emma, and Marie-Luise von Franz. *The Grail Legend.* 2d ed. Translated by Andrea Dykes. Princeton: Princeton University Press, 1998.

Oslchki, Leonardo. *The Grail Castle and Its Mysteries.* Translated by J. A. Scott. Manchester: University of Manchester Press, 1966.

Matthews, John. *The Elements of the Grail Tradition.* Rockport, MA: Element, 1996.

McConkie, Bruce R. *Doctrinal New Testament Commentary.* 3 vols. Salt Lake City: Bookcraft, 1965–73.

Parry, Donald W., and Dana M. Pike, eds. *LDS Perspectives on the Dead Sea Scrolls.* Provo, UT: Foundation for Ancient Research and Mormon Studies, 1997.

Robinson, James M. *The Gospel of Jesus: In Search of the Original "Good News."* New York: HarperSan Francisco, 2005.

Robinson, James M., ed. *The Nag Hammadi Library in English.* 3d rev. ed. San Francisco: Harper & Row, 1988.

Weston, Jessie L. *The Quest of the Holy Grail.* New York: Barnes and Noble, 1964.

Witherington III, Ben. *The Gospel Code: Novel Claims about Jesus, Mary Magdalene, and Da Vinci.* Downers Grove, IL: InterVarsity Press, 2004.

Index

About the Authors

Richard Neitzel Holzapfel

Richard Neitzel Holzapfel is the managing director of the Religious Studies Center publication office and professor of church history and doctrine at Brigham Young University. He received his Ph.D. in Ancient History at the University of California Irvine, and his current research focuses on ancient and modern scripture and Church history. Richard and his wife, Jeni, are the parents of five children and reside in Provo, Utah.

Andrew C. Skinner

Andrew C. Skinner serves as the director of the Neal A. Maxwell Institute for Religious Scholarship and professor of ancient scripture at Brigham Young University. He holds a master's degree in theology from Harvard University and a Ph.D. in history from the University of Denver and is the author or coauthor of numerous books on the New Testament, including *Verse by Verse, the Four Gospels* (2006). He and his wife, Janet, have six children and reside in Lindon, Utah.

Thomas A. Wayment

Thomas A. Wayment is an assistant professor of ancient scripture at Brigham Young University. He received his Ph.D. in New Testament Studies from Claremont Graduate University, and continues his research on the life of Jesus and the formation of the early Christian Church. He is the co-editor of three books on the ministry of Christ and the editor of *The Complete Joseph Smith Translation of the New Testament: A Side-by-Side Comparison with the King James Version* (2005). Thomas and his wife, Brandi, have two children.